SRA

Reading Mastery

Signature Edition

Spelling Presentation Book
Grade 1

Siegfried Engelmann
Elaine C. Bruner
Robert Dixon

W9-BSK-549

McGraw Hill **SRA**

Columbus, OH

READING MASTERY is a registered trademark of The McGraw-Hill Companies, Inc.

SRAonline.com

 SRA

Copyright © 2008 by SRA/McGraw-Hill.

All rights reserved. No part of this publication may be reproduced or distributed in any form or by any means, or stored in a database or retrieval system, without the prior written consent of The McGraw-Hill Companies, Inc., including, but not limited to, network storage or transmission, or broadcast for distance learning.

Printed in the United States of America.

Send all inquiries to this address:
SRA/McGraw-Hill
4400 Easton Commons
Columbus, OH 43219

ISBN: 978-0-07-612457-2
MHID: 0-07-612457-6

10 11 12 13 RMN 17 16 15 14

The **McGraw·Hill** Companies

Guide to *Spelling Presentation Book* Grade 1

Introduction

There are 160 lessons in the *Reading Mastery Signature Edition,* Grade 1 spelling program. In the first 90 spelling lessons, and in the first 79 lessons of the reading program, children spell by sounds rather than by letter names. Beginning with lesson 90 in the spelling program, after children have mastered letter names in the reading program, they begin to spell conventionally, using letter names.

Materials Needed

The materials required for the spelling program are this spelling presentation book, which contains detailed directions for presenting each lesson; lined paper and pencils for children to use; and a chalkboard or whiteboard for presenting some of the tasks.

Placement

Children can enter the spelling program at one of two lessons—1 or 11. Children who are placed at lesson 11 in the reading program begin at lesson 11 in the spelling program.

Scheduling

The amount of time required for each spelling lesson is approximately ten to fifteen minutes. Therefore, the spelling program can be used flexibly during a block of reading and language arts instruction.

The spelling program can be presented to either the entire class or small groups. Note that if the program is presented to the entire class, you begin with lesson 1 (unless all children in the class are scheduled to begin the reading program at lesson 11).

Skipping Lessons

If children in a group skip reading lessons on the basis of performance, they can skip the corresponding spelling lessons. In other words, if children skip reading lesson 38, they can also skip spelling lesson 38. In this way, you will be working with the same spelling lesson and reading lesson each day with a given group. Because some of the spelling concepts differ from the reading concepts, you should teach key concepts from any spelling lessons you might skip. For more information on skipping reading lessons, see the Teacher's Guide.

General Procedures

Give each child lined paper and a pencil. It is preferable for children to write dictated sounds, letters, and sentences in a row (across) instead of a column (down the paper). Children should write dictated words in a column.

Overview

Spelling by Sounds

Lessons 1 through 10 consist of a review of words that were presented in the Grade K spelling program. During these lessons, children write sounds from dictation. Children also write words after they say the sounds "the hard way," which means phonemically segmenting words with pauses between the sounds.

Beginning with lesson 11, children write sound combinations from dictation. The first sound combinations introduced are **ar** and **th.** Other combinations introduced in the program are **sh, ing, al, wh, er,** and **ck.**

Beginning in lesson 12, children write words that contain the sound combination **th** (introduced in lesson 11). You write words containing the sound combination **th** on the board. Children first read these words and say the sounds for each of the words. After you erase the board, children write the words.

After children have worked with a given sound combination for four lessons, they are introduced to an abbreviated format in which they say the sounds for a word and then write the word. (This format begins in lesson 14 with **th** words.)

Beginning at lesson 21, irregular words are introduced in the spelling program. In the introductory format, you present a variation of the irregular format used in reading: When you write the word **was,** you write these sounds: **www aaa sss.** Children say the sounds. Then they write the word.

After an irregular word has appeared in the introductory format for one or two lessons, it appears in an abbreviated format in which children say the sounds for the word (without your demonstration) and then write the word.

In lesson 15, children are introduced to a review format. The words that appear in this format are words that have appeared frequently in the preceding lessons or are new, easy, regular words. This format does not call for children to say the sounds in a word before writing it. Children are instructed to "think about the sounds in _____ and write the word."

Sentence writing is introduced in lesson 21. Children write one sentence during each lesson until lesson 36, at which time two sentences are introduced in each lesson.

The words used in sentence writing have been presented frequently and must have appeared in the review format. You say the sentence children are to write. Children repeat the sentence. Then they say it the slow way (with a pause between the words). After that, they write the sentence.

Spelling by Letter Names
(Lessons 91–160)
Children begin to spell conventionally by letter names beginning with lesson 91. In order to help you more easily differentiate sounds and letter names at a glance, the lesson style changes at lesson 91. For example, here is a sentence writing activity from lesson 90, before students spell by letter names:

SENTENCE WRITING
EXERCISE 4
Write two sentences

a. Listen to this sentence. **A big thing fell in the sand.**
Say that sentence. Get ready. (Signal.) *A big thing fell in the sand.*

b. Now you're going to say that sentence the slow way. Get ready. (Signal.) (Signal for each word as the children say:) *A* (pause) *big* (pause) *thing* (pause) *fell* (pause) *in* (pause) *the* (pause) *sand.*

c. Everybody, write the sentence. Spell each word the right way. ✔

d. (Repeat steps *a–c* for **A hen fell in the mud.**)

A similar activity in lesson 91, when children begin to spell by letter names, looks like this:

EXERCISE 4
SENTENCE WRITING

a. Listen to this sentence: **The map is red.**

b. Say that sentence. Get ready. (Signal.) *The map is red.*

c. Write the sentence. ✔

d. I'll spell each word. Check your work. Make an **X** next to any word you got wrong.

e. First word: **The. T-H-E.**

f. Next word: **map. M-A-P.**

g. (Repeat step *f* for **is, red.**)

Note that in the second example, you correct the sentences by spelling the words in those sentences using letter names. The letter names in the spelled words are represented with capital letters.

Initially in lessons 91–160, children spell words familiar from earlier lessons. Gradually, children expand their spelling vocabulary to more advanced spelling patterns and irregular words.

A unique activity in the spelling program not only contributes to improved spelling achievement, but also to fluent decoding. Here is an example taken from lesson 104:

EXERCISE 1
IDENTIFYING SPELLED WORDS

a. I'll spell some words. See if you can tell which word I spell.

b. Listen to this word: **M-A-P.**
- Listen again: **M-A-P.**
- What word? (Signal.) *Map.*

c. Listen to this word: **H-O-T.**
- Listen again: **H-O-T.**
- What word? (Signal.) *Hot.*

d. (Repeat step *c* for **me.**)

In this activity, children are essentially decoding words—based on hearing the names of letters, not seeing them. Initially, children are taught this skill in a much easier exercise. As they master the skill, the exercises become more challenging.

Phonemic segmentation (Say the Sounds) is a regular part of the spelling lessons. Segmenting words phonemically doesn't absolutely guarantee that children will spell accurately, but it helps greatly reduce the variety of misspellings that children sometimes produce without the benefit of learning phonemic segmentation.

Important Information

1. The spelling program does not rely on joined letters or macrons (long lines over long vowels). Children are not to write either joined letters or macrons. Children also do not write capital letters until lesson 97.

2. If an **e** appears on the end of a word while students are spelling by sounds (lesson 39 **come,** lesson 62), call the sound **ēēē** when sounding out the word (not **eee** as in **end**). Spelling by letter names comes easier to children if they are used to referring to the **e**'s on the end of words by the letter name.

3. In lessons 1–90, if a vowel in a word is long, say the long vowel sound when sounding out the word.

Examples:

The **o** in **over** would be **ōōō** (since it is pronounced long in the word).

The first **e** in **ever** would be **eee** (since it is not pronounced long in the word).

The **o** in **not** would be short: **ooo.**
The **o** in **no** would be long: **ōōō.**

General Correction Procedures

If children make mistakes, follow the correction procedure of (1) model and (2) test.

If you ask children to say the sounds in the word **man,** and they make mistakes:
1. (Model) Here are the sounds in **man.** Listen. **mmm** (pause) **aaa** (pause) **nnn.**
2. (Test) Your turn. Say the sounds in **man.** (Tap for each sound as children say:) *mmm* (pause) *aaa* (pause) *nnn.*

If a child makes a mistake when you ask children to think about the sounds in the word **stop** and write the word:
1. (Model) Here are the sounds in the word **stop.** Listen. **sss** (pause) **t** (pause) **ooo** (pause) **p.**
2. (Test) Your turn. Say the sounds in **stop.** (Tap for each sound as children say:) *sss* (pause) *t* (pause) *ooo* (pause) *p.*
3. (Delayed test) Think about the sounds in **stop** and write the word. ✔

If a child misspells a word using letter names:
1. (Model) Listen: **M-A-N.**
2. (Test) Your turn. Spell **man.** Get ready. (Signal.) *M-A-N.*
3. (Delayed test) Again. Spell **man.** Get ready. (Signal.) *M-A-N.*

Summary of Skills Taught

At the end of the spelling program, children can spell regular words and some irregular words by sounds and write the words accurately. They can spell by sounds and letter names words that contain common sound combinations, such as **ar, al, sh, th,** and **wh.** They can accurately spell words in a variety of simple sentence forms, including questions and some fairly long statements.

SECTION 1
Spelling by Sounds
Lessons 1–90

LESSON

Note: Children who are placed at lesson 1 in the reading program begin at lesson 1 in the spelling program.

SOUND WRITING
EXERCISE 1

Write **h, s, a, r, e, t**

a. You're going to write some sounds.
b. Here's the first sound you're going to write. Listen. **h.** What sound? (Signal.) *h.*
c. Write **h.** ✔
d. Next sound. Listen. **sss.** What sound? (Signal.) *sss.*
e. Write **sss.** ✔
f. (Repeat steps *d* and *e* for **a, r, e,** and **t.**)

WORD WRITING
EXERCISE 2

Read, say the sounds, write **rat**

a. (Write **rat** on the board.)
b. Everybody, read this word the fast way. Get ready. (Signal.) *Rat.*
• What word? (Signal.) *Rat.* Yes, **rat.**
c. My turn to say the sounds in **rat** the hard way. (Touch each sound.) **rrr** (pause) **aaa** (pause) **t.**
d. Your turn. Say the sounds in **rat** the hard way. Get ready. (Touch each sound as children say:) *rrr* (pause) *aaa* (pause) *t.*
e. (Erase **rat.**) I'll tap for each sound. You say the sounds in **rat** the hard way. Get ready. (Tap for each sound as children say:) *rrr* (pause) *aaa* (pause) *t.*
• (Repeat until firm.)
f. Everybody, write the word (pause) **rat.** ✔

EXERCISE 3

Read, say the sounds, write **sat**

a. (Write **sat** on the board.)
b. Everybody, read this word the fast way. Get ready. (Signal.) *Sat.*
• What word? (Signal.) *Sat.* Yes, **sat.**
c. My turn to say the sounds in **sat** the hard way. (Touch each sound.) **sss** (pause) **aaa** (pause) **t.**
d. Your turn. Say the sounds in **sat** the hard way. Get ready. (Touch each sound as children say:) *sss* (pause) *aaa* (pause) *t.*
e. (Erase **sat.**) I'll tap for each sound. You say the sounds in **sat** the hard way. Get ready. (Tap for each sound as children say:) *sss* (pause) *aaa* (pause) *t.*
• (Repeat until firm.)
f. Everybody, write the word (pause) **sat.** ✔

EXERCISE 4

Read, say the sounds, write **hat**

a. (Write **hat** on the board.)
b. Everybody, read this word the fast way. Get ready. (Signal.) *Hat.*
• What word? (Signal.) *Hat.* Yes, **hat.**
c. My turn to say the sounds in **hat** the hard way. (Touch each sound.) **h** (pause) **aaa** (pause) **t.**
d. Your turn. Say the sounds in **hat** the hard way. Get ready. (Touch each sound as children say:) *h* (pause) *aaa* (pause) *t.*
e. (Erase **hat.**) I'll tap for each sound. You say the sounds in **hat** the hard way. Get ready. (Tap for each sound as children say:) *h* (pause) *aaa* (pause) *t.*
• (Repeat until firm.)
f. Everybody, write the word (pause) **hat.** ✔

EXERCISE 5

Read, say the sounds, write **he**

a. (Write **he** on the board.)
b. Everybody, read this word the fast way. Get ready. (Signal.) *He.*
• What word? (Signal.) *He.* Yes, **he.**

c. My turn to say the sounds in **he** the hard way. (Touch each sound.) **h** (pause) ēēē.

d. Your turn. Say the sounds in **he** the hard way. Get ready. (Touch each sound as children say:) *h* (pause) *ēēē.*

e. (Erase **he.**) I'll tap for each sound. You say the sounds in **he** the hard way. Get ready. (Tap for each sound as children say:) *h* (pause) *ēēē.*

- (Repeat until firm.)

f. Everybody, write the word (pause) **he.** ✔

LESSON 2

SOUND WRITING
EXERCISE 1

Write **h, s, r, a, e, t**

a. You're going to write some sounds.

b. Here's the first sound you're going to write. Listen. **h.** What sound? (Signal.) *h.*

c. Write **h.** ✔

d. Next sound. Listen. **sss.** What sound? (Signal.) *sss.*

e. Write **sss.** ✔

f. (Repeat steps *d* and *e* for **r, a, e,** and **t.**)

WORD WRITING
EXERCISE 2

Read, say the sounds, write **he, hat, sat**

a. (Write **he** on the board.)

b. Everybody, read this word the fast way. Get ready. (Signal.) *He.*

- What word? (Signal.) *He.* Yes, **he.**

c. My turn to say the sounds in **he** the hard way. (Touch each sound.) **h** (pause) ēēē.

d. Your turn. Say the sounds in **he** the hard way. Get ready. (Touch each sound as children say:) *h* (pause) *ēēē.*

e. (Erase **he.**) I'll tap for each sound. You say the sounds in **he** the hard way. Get ready. (Tap for each sound as children say:) *h* (pause) *ēēē.*

- (Repeat until firm.)

f. Everybody, write the word (pause) **he.** ✔

g. (Repeat steps *a–f* for **hat** and **sat.**)

EXERCISE 3

Read, say the sounds, write **rat**

a. (Write **rat** on the board.)

b. Everybody, read this word the fast way. Get ready. (Signal.) *Rat.*

- What word? (Signal.) *Rat.* Yes, **rat.**

c. Say the sounds in **rat** the hard way. (Touch each sound as the children say:) *rrr* (pause) *aaa* (pause) *t.*

d. (Erase **rat.**) I'll tap for each sound. You say the sounds in **rat** the hard way. Get ready. (Tap for each sound as the children say:) *rrr* (pause) *aaa* (pause) *t.*

- (Repeat until firm.)

e. Everybody, write the word (pause) **rat.** ✔

LESSON 3

SOUND WRITING
EXERCISE 1

Write **a, h, m, e, t, s**

a. You're going to write some sounds.

b. Here's the first sound you're going to write. Listen. **aaa.** What sound? (Signal.) *aaa.*

c. Write **aaa.** ✔

d. Next sound. Listen. **h.** What sound? (Signal.) *h.*

e. Write **h.** ✔

f. (Repeat steps *d* and *e* for **m, e, t,** and **s.**)

WORD WRITING
EXERCISE 2

Read, say the sounds, write **me, mat**

a. (Write **me** on the board.)

b. Everybody, read this word the fast way. Get ready. (Signal.) *Me.*

- What word? (Signal.) *Me.* Yes, **me.**

c. My turn to say the sounds in **me** the hard way. (Touch each sound.) **mmm** (pause) ēēē.

d. Your turn. Say the sounds in **me** the hard way. Get ready. (Touch each sound as children say:) *mmm* (pause) *ēēē.*

e. (Erase **me**.) I'll tap for each sound. You say the sounds in **me** the hard way. Get ready. (Tap for each sound as children say:) *mmm* (pause) *ēēē.*
- (Repeat until firm.)
f. Everybody, write the word (pause) **me.** ✔
g. (Repeat steps *a–f* for **mat.**)

EXERCISE 3

Read, say the sounds, write **sam, sat**

Children are not responsible for capital letters.

a. (Write **sam** on the board.)
b. Everybody, read this word the fast way. Get ready. (Signal.) *Sam.*
- What word? (Signal.) *Sam.* Yes, **sam.**
c. Say the sounds in **sam** the hard way. (Touch each sound as the children say:) *sss* (pause) *aaa* (pause) *mmm.*
d. (Erase **sam**.) I'll tap for each sound. You say the sounds in **sam** the hard way. Get ready. (Tap for each sound as the children say:) *sss* (pause) *aaa* (pause) *mmm.*
- (Repeat until firm.)
e. Everybody, write the word (pause) **sam.** ✔
f. (Repeat steps *a–e* for **sat.**)

LESSON 4

SOUND WRITING
EXERCISE 1

Write **m, r, n, a, t, e**

a. You're going to write some sounds.
b. Here's the first sound you're going to write. Listen. **mmm.** What sound? (Signal.) *mmm.*
c. Write **mmm.** ✔
d. Next sound. Listen. **rrr.** What sound? (Signal.) *rrr.*
e. Write **rrr.** ✔
f. (Repeat steps *d* and *e* for **n, a, t,** and **e.**)

WORD WRITING
EXERCISE 2

Read, say the sounds, write **ram**

a. (Write **ram** on the board.)
b. Everybody, read this word the fast way. Get ready. (Signal.) *Ram.*
- What word? (Signal.) *Ram.* Yes, **ram.**
c. My turn to say the sounds in **ram** the hard way. (Touch each sound.) **rrr** (pause) **aaa** (pause) **mmm.**
d. Your turn. Say the sounds in **ram** the hard way. Get ready. (Touch each sound as children say:) *rrr* (pause) *aaa* (pause) *mmm.*
e. (Erase **ram**.) I'll tap for each sound. You say the sounds in **ram** the hard way. Get ready. (Tap for each sound as children say:) *rrr* (pause) *aaa* (pause) *mmm.*
- (Repeat until firm.)
f. Everybody, write the word (pause) **ram.** ✔

EXERCISE 3

Read, say the sounds, write **sam, mat**

a. (Write **sam** on the board.)
b. Everybody, read this word the fast way. Get ready. (Signal.) *Sam.*
- What word? (Signal.) *Sam.* Yes, **sam.**
c. Say the sounds in **sam** the hard way. (Touch each sound as the children say:) *sss* (pause) *aaa* (pause) *mmm.*
d. (Erase **sam**.) I'll tap for each sound. You say the sounds in **sam** the hard way. Get ready. (Tap for each sound as the children say:) *sss* (pause) *aaa* (pause) *mmm.*
- (Repeat until firm.)
e. Everybody, write the word (pause) **sam.** ✔
f. (Repeat steps *a–e* for **mat.**)

EXERCISE 4

Say the sounds, write **me**

a. You're going to write the word (pause) **me.** Say the sounds in **me.** Get ready. (Tap for each sound as the children say:) *mmm* (pause) *ēēē.*

b. Everybody, write the word (pause) **me.** ✔

EXERCISE 5

Listen, say the sounds, write **see**

a. You're going to write the word (pause) **see.** When you write the word **see,** you write these sounds: **sss** (pause) *ēēē* (pause) *ēēē.*

b. Say the sounds you write for (pause) **see.** Get ready. (Tap for each sound as the children say:) *sss* (pause) *ēēē* (pause) *ēēē.*

• (Repeat until firm.)

c. Everybody, write the word (pause) **see.** ✔

LESSON 5

SOUND WRITING
EXERCISE 1

Write **f, t, h, r, m, e, s**

a. You're going to write some sounds.

b. Here's the first sound you're going to write. Listen. **fff.** What sound? (Signal.) *fff.*

c. Write **fff.** ✔

d. Next sound. Listen. **t.** What sound? (Signal.) *t.*

e. Write **t.** ✔

f. (Repeat steps *d* and *e* for **h, r, m, e,** and **s.**)

WORD WRITING
EXERCISE 2

Read, say the sounds, write **see, at, am**

a. (Write **see** on the board.)

b. Everybody, read this word the fast way. Get ready. (Signal.) *See.*

• What word? (Signal.) *See.* Yes, **see.**

c. Say the sounds in **see** the hard. (Touch each sound as the children say:) *sss* (pause) *ēēē* (pause) *ēēē.*

d. (Erase **see.**) I'll tap for each sound. You say the sounds in **see** the hard way. Get ready. (Tap for each sound as the children say:) *sss* (pause) *ēēē* (pause) *ēēē.*

• (Repeat until firm.)

e. Everybody, write the word (pause) **see.** ✔

f. (Repeat steps *a–e* for **at** and **am.**)

EXERCISE 3

Say the sounds, write **ram, ham**

a. You're going to write the word (pause) **ram.** Say the sounds in **ram.** Get ready. (Tap for each sound as the children say:) *rrr* (pause) *aaa* (pause) *mmm.*

• (Repeat until firm.)

b. Everybody, write the word (pause) **ram.** ✔

c. (Repeat steps *a* and *b* for **ham.**)

LESSON 6

SOUND WRITING
EXERCISE 1

Write **a, f, r, t, h, e**

a. You're going to write some sounds.

b. Here's the first sound you're going to write. Listen. **aaa.** What sound? (Signal.) *aaa.*

c. Write **aaa.** ✔

d. Next sound. Listen. **fff.** What sound? (Signal.) *fff.*

e. Write **fff.** ✔

f. (Repeat steps *d* and *e* for **r, t, h,** and **e.**)

WORD WRITING
EXERCISE 2

Read, say the sounds, write **see, fat**

a. (Write **see** on the board.)

b. Everybody, read this word the fast way. Get ready. (Signal.) *See.*

• What word? (Signal.) *See.* Yes, **see.**

c. Say the sounds in **see** the hard way. (Touch each sound as the children say:) *sss* (pause) *ēēē* (pause) *ēēē.*

d. (Erase **see.**) I'll tap for each sound. You say the sounds in **see** the hard way. Get ready. (Tap for each sound as the children say:) *sss* (pause) *ēēē* (pause) *ēēē.*

• (Repeat until firm.)

5

e. Everybody, write the word (pause) **see.** ✔

f. (Repeat steps *a–e* for **fat.**)

EXERCISE 3

Say the sounds, write **am, ham, ram**

a. You're going to write the word (pause) **am.** Say the sounds in **am.** Get ready. (Tap for each sound as the children say:) *aaa* (pause) *mmm.*

• (Repeat until firm.)

b. Everybody, write the word (pause) **am.** ✔

c. (Repeat steps *a* and *b* for **ham** and **ram.**)

LESSON 7

SOUND WRITING
EXERCISE 1

Write **h, r, a, f, t, e, s**

a. You're going to write some sounds.

b. Here's the first sound you're going to write. Listen. **h.** What sound? (Signal.) *h.*

c. Write **h.** ✔

d. Next sound. Listen. **rrr.** What sound? (Signal.) *rrr.*

e. Write **rrr.** ✔

f. (Repeat steps *d* and *e* for **a, f, t, e,** and **s.**)

WORD WRITING
EXERCISE 2

Say the sounds, write **he, me, see, mat, am, at**

a. You're going to write the word (pause) **he.** Say the sounds in **he.** Get ready. (Tap for each sound as the children say:) *h* (pause) *ē ē ē.*

• (Repeat until firm.)

b. Everybody, write the word (pause) **he.** ✔

c. (Repeat steps *a* and *b* for **me, see, mat, am,** and **at.**)

LESSON 8

SOUND WRITING
EXERCISE 1

Write **i, a, e, f, m, h, t**

a. You're going to write some sounds.

b. Here's the first sound you're going to write. Listen. **iii.** What sound? (Signal.) *iii.*

c. Write **iii.** ✔

d. Next sound. Listen. **aaa.** What sound? (Signal.) *aaa.*

e. Write **aaa.** ✔

f. (Repeat steps *d* and *e* for **e, f, m, h,** and **t.**)

WORD WRITING
EXERCISE 2

Say the sounds, write **me, am, ram, at, sat, fat**

a. You're going to write the word (pause) **me.** Say the sounds in **me.** Get ready. (Tap for each sound as the children say:) *mmm* (pause) *ē ē ē.*

• (Repeat until firm.)

b. Everybody, write the word (pause) **me.** ✔

c. (Repeat steps *a* and *b* for **am, ram, at, sat** and **fat.**)

LESSON 9

SOUND WRITING
EXERCISE 1

Write **i, f, e, s, a, h**

a. You're going to write some sounds.

b. Here's the first sound you're going to write. Listen. **iii.** What sound? (Signal.) *iii.*

c. Write **iii.** ✔

d. Next sound. Listen. **fff.** What sound? (Signal.) *fff.*

e. Write **fff.** ✔

f. (Repeat steps *d* and *e* for **e, s, a,** and **h.**)

WORD WRITING
EXERCISE 2

Read, say the sounds, write **it, fit**

a. (Write **it** on the board.)
b. Everybody, read this word the fast way. Get ready. (Signal.) *It.*
• What word? (Signal.) *It.* Yes, **it.**
c. Say the sounds in **it** the hard way. (Touch each sound as the children say:) *iii* (pause) *t.*
d. (Erase **it.**) I'll tap for each sound. You say the sounds in **it** the hard way. Get ready. (Tap for each sound as the children say:) *iii* (pause) *t.*
• (Repeat until firm.)
e. Everybody, write the word (pause) **it.**
f. (Repeat steps *a–e* for **fit.**)

EXERCISE 3

Say the sounds, write **ham, at, hat, fat**

a. You're going to write the word (pause) **ham.** Say the sounds in **ham.** Get ready. (Tap for each sound as the children say:) *h* (pause) *aaa* (pause) *mmm.*
• (Repeat until firm.)
b. Everybody, write the word (pause) **ham.**
c. (Repeat steps *a* and *b* for **at, hat,** and **fat.**)

LESSON 10

SOUND WRITING
EXERCISE 1

Write **i, e, a, t, s, m, f**

a. You're going to write some sounds.
b. Here's the first sound you're going to write. Listen. **iii.** What sound? (Signal.) *iii.*
c. Write **iii.** ✔
d. Next sound. Listen. **eee.** What sound? (Signal.) *eee.*
e. Write **eee.** ✔
f. (Repeat steps *d* and *e* for **a, t, s, m,** and **f.**)

WORD WRITING
EXERCISE 2

Read, say the sounds, write **if, it**

a. (Write **if** on the board.)
b. Everybody, read this word the fast way. Get ready. (Signal.) *If.*
• What word? (Signal.) *If.* Yes, **if.**
c. Say the sounds in **if** the hard way. (Touch each sound as the children say:) *iii* (pause) *fff.*
d. (Erase **if.**) I'll tap for each sound. You say the sounds in **if** the hard way. Get ready. (Tap for each sound as the children say:) *iii* (pause) *fff.*
• (Repeat until firm.)
e. Everybody, write the word (pause) **if.** ✔
f. (Repeat steps *a–e* for **it.**)

EXERCISE 3

Say the sounds, write **sit, see, me, at, am**

a. You're going to write the word (pause) **sit.** Say the sounds in **sit.** Get ready. (Tap for each sound as the children say:) *sss* (pause) *iii* (pause) *t.*
• (Repeat until firm.)
b. Everybody, write the word (pause) **sit.** ✔
c. (Repeat steps *a* and *b* for **see, me, at,** and **am.**)

LESSON 11

Note: Children who are placed at lesson 11 in the reading program begin at spelling lesson 11.

SOUND WRITING
EXERCISE 1

Write **a, h, i, s, e**

a. You're going to write some sounds.
b. Here's the first sound you're going to write. Listen. **aaa.** What sound? (Signal.) *aaa.*
c. Write **aaa.** ✔
d. Next sound. Listen. **h.** What sound? (Signal.) *h.*
e. Write **h.** ✔
f. (Repeat steps *d* and *e* for **i, s,** and **e.**)

EXERCISE 2

Introduce sound combination th

a. (Write on the board: **th.**)
b. (Point to **th.**) Everybody, tell me the sound these letters make. Get ready. (Signal.) *th.* Yes, **th.**
c. (Erase **th.**) Everybody, write the letters that go together and make the sound **th.** ✔

WORD WRITING
EXERCISE 3

Read, say the sounds, write **sit, rat**

a. (Write **sit** on the board.)
b. Everybody, read this word the fast way. Get ready.
   (Signal.) *Sit.*
• What word? (Signal.) *Sit.* Yes, **sit.**
c. My turn to say the sounds in **sit** the hard way. (Touch each sound.) *sss* (pause) *iii* (pause) *t.*
d. Your turn. Say the sounds in **sit** the hard way. Get ready. (Touch each sound as children say:) *sss* (pause) *iii* (pause) *t.*
e. (Erase **sit.**) I'll tap for each sound. You say the sounds in **sit** the hard way. Get ready. (Tap for each sound as children say:) *sss* (pause) *iii* (pause) *t.*
• (Repeat until firm.)
f. Everybody, write the word (pause) **sit.** ✔
g. (Repeat steps *a–f* for **rat.**)

EXERCISE 4

Read, say the sounds, write **man, fit, he**

a. (Write **man** on the board.)
b. Everybody, read this word the fast way. Get ready. (Signal.) *Man.*
• What word? (Signal.) *Man.* Yes, **man.**
c. Say the sounds in **man** the hard way. (Touch each sound as the children say:) *mmm* (pause) *aaa* (pause) *nnn.*
d. (Erase **man.**) I'll tap for each sound. You say the sounds in **man** the hard way. Get ready. (Tap for each sound as the children say:) *mmm* (pause) *aaa* (pause) *nnn.*
• (Repeat until firm.)

e. Everybody, write the word (pause) **man.** ✔
f. (Repeat steps *a–e* for **fit** and **he.**)

LESSON 12

SOUND WRITING
EXERCISE 1

Write **e, m, a, s, i**

a. You're going to write some sounds.
b. Here's the first sound you're going to write. Listen. **eee.** What sound? (Signal.) *eee.*
c. Write **eee.** ✔
d. Next sound. Listen. **mmm.** What sound? (Signal.) *mmm.*
e. Write **mmm.** ✔
f. (Repeat steps *d* and *e* for **a, s,** and **i.**)

WORD WRITING
EXERCISE 2

Read, say the sounds, write **rat**

a. (Write **rat** on the board.)
b. Everybody, read this word the fast way. Get ready. (Signal.) *Rat.*
• What word? (Signal.) *Rat.* Yes, **rat.**
c. My turn to say the sounds in **rat** the hard way. (Touch each sound.) *rrr* (pause) *aaa* (pause) *t.*
d. Your turn. Say the sounds in **rat** the hard way. Get ready. (Touch each sound as children say:) *rrr* (pause) *aaa* (pause) *t.*
e. (Erase **rat.**) I'll tap for each sound. You say the sounds in **rat** the hard way. Get ready. (Tap for each sound as children say:) *rrr* (pause) *aaa* (pause) *t.*
• (Repeat until firm.)
f. Everybody, write the word (pause) **rat.** ✔

EXERCISE 3

Read, say the sounds, write **sit, fit**

a. (Write **sit** on the board.)
b. Everybody, read this word the fast way. Get ready. (Signal.) *Sit.*
• What word? (Signal.) *Sit.* Yes, **sit.**

c. Say the sounds in **sit** the hard way. (Touch each sound as the children say:) *sss* (pause) *iii* (pause) *t.*

d. (Erase **sit**.) I'll tap for each sound. You say the sounds in **sit** the hard way. Get ready. (Tap for each sound as the children say:) *sss* (pause) *iii* (pause) *t.*

  • (Repeat until firm.)

e. Everybody, write the word (pause) **sit**. ✔

f. (Repeat steps *a–e* for **fit**.)

SOUND WRITING
EXERCISE 4

Introduce sound combination **th**

a. (Write on the board: **th**.)

b. (Point to **th**.) Everybody, tell me the sound these letters make. Get ready. (Signal.) *th*. Yes, **th**.

c. (Erase **th**.) Everybody, write the letters that go together and make the sound **th**. ✔

WORD WRITING
EXERCISE 5

Write sound combination words **this, that, the, them**

a. (Write on the board: **this, that, the, them**.)

b. (Point to **this**.) Everybody, read this word the fast way. Get ready. (Signal.) *This.* Yes, **this**.

c. Everybody, say the sounds you write for the word (pause) **this**. Get ready. (Touch **th, i, s** as the children say:) *th* (pause) *iii* (pause) *sss.*

  • (Repeat until firm.)

d. (Erase **this**.) Everybody, write the word (pause) **this**. ✔

e. (Point to **that**.) Everybody, read this word the fast way. Get ready. (Signal.) *That.* Yes, **that**.

f. Everybody, say the sounds you write for the word (pause) **that**. Get ready. (Touch **th, a, t** as the children say:) *th* (pause) *aaa* (pause) *t.*

  • (Repeat until firm.)

g. (Erase **that**.) Everybody, write the word (pause) **that**. ✔

h. (Point to **the**.) Everybody, read this word the fast way. Get ready. (Signal.) *The.* Yes, **the**.

i. Everybody, say the sounds you write for the word (pause) **the**. Get ready. (Touch **th, e** as the children say:) *th* (pause) *ēēē.*

  • (Repeat until firm.)

j. (Erase **the**.) Everybody, write the word (pause) **the**. ✔

k. (Point to **them**.) Everybody, read this word the fast way. Get ready. (Signal.) *Them.* Yes, **them**.

l. Everybody, say the sounds you write for the word (pause) **them**. Get ready. (Touch **th, e, m** as the children say:) *th* (pause) *eee* (pause) *mmm.*

m. (Erase **them**.) Everybody, write the word (pause) **them**. ✔

LESSON 13

SOUND WRITING
EXERCISE 1

Write **a, h, i, s, e**

a. You're going to write some sounds.

b. Here's the first sound you're going to write. Listen. **aaa**. What sound? (Signal.) *aaa.*

c. Write **aaa**. ✔

d. Next sound. Listen. **h**. What sound? (Signal.) *h.*

e. Write **h**. ✔

f. (Repeat steps *d* and *e* for **i, s,** and **e**.)

EXERCISE 2

Introduce sound combination **th**

a. (Write on the board: **th**.)

b. (Point to **th**.) Everybody, tell me the sound these letters make. Get ready. (Signal.) *th*. Yes, **th**.

c. (Erase **th**.) Everybody, write the letters that go together and make the sound **th**. ✔

9

WORD WRITING
EXERCISE 3

Write sound combination words **that, the, this, them**

a. (Write on the board: **that, the, this, them.**)

b. (Point to **that.**) Everybody, read this word the fast way. Get ready. (Signal.) *That.* Yes, **that.**

c. Everybody, say the sounds you write for the word (pause) **that.** Get ready. (Touch **th, a, t** as the children say:) *th* (pause) *aaa* (pause) *t.*

• (Repeat until firm.)

d. (Erase **that.**) Everybody, write the word (pause) **that.** ✔

e. (Point to **the.**) Everybody, read this word the fast way. Get ready. (Signal.) *The.* Yes, **the.**

f. Everybody, say the sounds you write for the word (pause) **the.** Get ready. (Touch **th, e** as the children say:) *th* (pause) *ēēē.*

• (Repeat until firm.)

g. (Erase **the.**) Everybody, write the word (pause) **the.** ✔

h. (Point to **this.**) Everybody, read this word the fast way. Get ready. (Signal.) *This.* Yes, **this.**

i. Everybody, say the sounds you write for the word (pause) **this.** Get ready. (Touch **th, i, s** as the children say:) *th* (pause) *iii* (pause) *sss.*

• (Repeat until firm.)

j. (Erase **this.**) Everybody, write the word (pause) **this.** ✔

k. (Point to **them.**) Everybody, read this word the fast way. Get ready. (Signal.) *Them.* Yes, **them.**

l. Everybody, say the sounds you write for the word (pause) **them.** Get ready. (Touch **th, e, m** as the children say:) *th* (pause) *eee* (pause) *mmm.*

• (Repeat until firm.)

m. (Erase **them.**) Everybody, write the word (pause) **them.** ✔

EXERCISE 4

Say the sounds, write **he, me, hat, hit**

a. You're going to write the word (pause) **he.** Say the sounds in **he.** Get ready. (Tap for each sound as the children say:) *h* (pause) *ēēē.*

• (Repeat until firm.)

b. Everybody, write the word (pause) **he.** ✔

c. (Repeat steps *a* and *b* for **me, hat,** and **hit.**)

LESSON 14

SOUND WRITING
EXERCISE 1

Write **r, t, f**

a. You're going to write some sounds.

b. Here's the first sound you're going to write. Listen. **rrr.** What sound? (Signal.) *rrr.*

c. Write **rrr.** ✔

d. Next sound. Listen. **t.** What sound? (Signal.) *t.*

e. Write **t.** ✔

f. (Repeat steps *d* and *e* for **f.**)

EXERCISE 2

Write **th**

a. Everybody, you're going to write the letters that go together and make the sound **th.** What sound? (Signal.) *th.*

b. Write **th.** ✔

WORD WRITING
EXERCISE 3

Write sound combination words **the, them, that, this**

a. (Write on the board: **the, them, that, this**)

b. (Point to **the.**) Everybody, read this word the fast way. Get ready. (Signal.) *The.* Yes, **the.**

c. Everybody, say the sounds you write for the word (pause) **the.** Get ready. (Touch **th, e** as the children say:) *th* (pause) *ēēē.*
- (Repeat until firm.)
d. (Erase **the.**) Everybody, write the word (pause) **the.** ✔
e. (Repeat steps *b–d* for **them, that,** and **this.**)

EXERCISE 4

Say the sounds, write **ran, him, he, we, fan**

a. You're going to write the word (pause) **ran.** Say the sounds in **ran.** Get ready. (Tap for each sound as the children say:) *rrr* (pause) *aaa* (pause) *nnn.*
- (Repeat until firm.)
b. Everybody, write the word (pause) **ran.** ✔
c. (Repeat steps *a* and *b* for **him, he, we,** and **fan.**)

SOUND WRITING
EXERCISE 1

Write **f, t, d**

a. You're going to write some sounds.
b. Here's the first sound you're going to write. Listen. **fff.** What sound? (Signal.) *fff.*
c. Write **fff.** ✔
d. Next sound. Listen. **t.** What sound? (Signal.) *t.*
e. Write **t.** ✔
f. (Repeat steps *d* and *e* for **d.**)

EXERCISE 2

Write **th**

a. Everybody, you're going to write the letters that go together and make the sound **th.** What sound? (Signal.) *th.*
b. Write **th.** ✔

WORD WRITING
EXERCISE 3

Write sound combination words **them, this, that, the**

a. (Write on the board: **them, this, that, the.**)
b. (Point to **them.**) Everybody, read this word the fast way. Get ready. (Signal.) *Them.* Yes, **them.**
c. Everybody, say the sounds you write for the word (pause) **them.** Get ready. (Touch **th, e, m** as the children say:) *th* (pause) *eee* (pause) *mmm.*
- (Repeat until firm.)
d. (Erase **them.**) Everybody, write the word (pause) **them.** ✔
e. (Repeat steps *b–d* for **this, that,** and **the.**)

EXERCISE 4

Say the sounds, write **fit, we**

a. You're going to write the word (pause) **fit.** Say the sounds in **fit.** Get ready. (Tap for each sound as the children say:) *fff* (pause) *iii* (pause) *t.*
- (Repeat until firm.)
b. Everybody, write the word (pause) **fit.** ✔
c. (Repeat steps *a* and *b* for **we.**)

EXERCISE 5

Write **fat, him, ham**

a. You're going to write the word (pause) **fat.** Think about the sounds in **fat** and write the word. ✔
b. (Repeat step *a* for **him** and **ham.**)

LESSON 16

SOUND WRITING
EXERCISE 1

Write **d, p, t, f**

a. You're going to write some sounds.
b. Here's the first sound you're going to write. Listen. **d.** What sound? (Signal.) *d.*

11

c. Write **d.** ✔

d. Next sound. Listen. **p.** What sound? (Signal.) *p.*

e. Write **p.** ✔

f. (Repeat steps *d* and *e* for **t** and **f.**)

EXERCISE 2

Write **th**

a. Everybody, you're going to write the letters that go together and make the sound **th.** What sound? (Signal.) *th.*

b. Write **th.** ✔

WORD WRITING
EXERCISE 3

Say the sounds, write **he, that, fan, fin**

a. You're going to write the word (pause) **he.** Say the sounds in **he.** Get ready. (Tap for each sound as the children say:) *h* (pause) *ēēē.*

• (Repeat until firm.)

b. Everybody, write the word (pause) **he.** ✔

c. (Repeat steps *a* and *b* for **that, fan,** and **fin.**)

EXERCISE 4

Write **me, this, him, ham, mat, sat, sit**

a. You're going to write the word (pause) **me.** Think about the sounds in **me** and write the word. ✔

b. (Repeat step *a* for **this, him, ham, mat, sat,** and **sit.**)

LESSON **17**

SOUND WRITING
EXERCISE 1

Write **r, d, p, g**

a. You're going to write some sounds.

b. Here's the first sound you're going to write. Listen. **rrr.** What sound? (Signal.) *rrr.*

c. Write **rrr.** ✔

d. Next sound. Listen. **d.** What sound? (Signal.) *d.*

e. Write **d.** ✔

f. (Repeat steps *d* and *e* for **p** and **g.**)

EXERCISE 2

Introduce sound combination **ar**

a. (Write on the board: **ar.**)

b. (Point to **ar.**) Everybody, tell me the sound these letters make. Get ready. (Signal.) *Are.* Yes, **are.**

c. (Erase **ar.**) Everybody, write the two letters that go together and make the sound **ar.** ✔

WORD WRITING
EXERCISE 3

Write sound combination words **far, tar, car**

a. (Write on the board: **far, tar, car.**)

b. (Point to **far.**) Everybody, read this word the fast way. Get ready. (Signal.) *Far.* Yes, **far.**

c. Everybody, say the sounds you write for the word (pause) **far.** Get ready. (Touch **f, ar** as the children say:) *fff* (pause) *ar.*

• (Repeat until firm.)

d. (Erase **far.**) Everybody, write the word (pause) **far.** ✔

e. (Repeat steps *b–d* for **tar** and **car.**)

EXERCISE 4

Say the sounds, write **that, this, the**

a. You're going to write the word (pause) **that.** Say the sounds in **that.** Get ready. (Tap for each sound as the children say:) *th* (pause) *aaa* (pause) *t.*

• (Repeat until firm.)

b. Everybody, write the word (pause) **that.** ✔

c. (Repeat steps *a* and *b* for **this** and **the.**)

EXERCISE 5

Write **ham, him, me, sit, sat**

a. You're going to write the word (pause) **ham.** Think about the sounds in **ham** and write the word. ✔

b. (Repeat step *a* for **him, me, sit,** and **sat.**)

LESSON 18

SOUND WRITING
EXERCISE 1

Write **m, n, b, g**

a. You're going to write some sounds.
b. Here's the first sound you're going to write. Listen. **mmm.** What sound? (Signal.) *mmm.*
c. Write **mmm.** ✔
d. Next sound. Listen. **nnn.** What sound? (Signal.) *nnn.*
e. Write **nnn.** ✔
f. (Repeat steps *d* and *e* for **b** and **g.**)

EXERCISE 2

Introduce sound combination **ar**

a. (Write on the board: **ar.**)
b. (Point to **ar.**) Everybody, tell me the sound these letters make. Get ready. (Signal.) *Are.* Yes, **are.**
c. (Erase **ar.**) Everybody, write the two letters that go together and make the sound **ar.** ✔

WORD WRITING
EXERCISE 3

Write sound combination words **bar, barn, far, farm**

a. (Write on the board: **bar, barn, far, farm.**)
b. (Point to **bar.**) Everybody, read this word the fast way. Get ready. (Signal.) *Bar.* Yes, **bar.**
c. Everybody, say the sounds you write for the word (pause) **bar.** Get ready. (Touch **b, ar** as the children say:) *b* (pause) *ar.*
• (Repeat until firm.)
d. (Erase **bar.**) Everybody, write the word (pause) **bar.** ✔
e. (Repeat steps *b–d* for **barn, far,** and **farm.**)

EXERCISE 4

Say the sounds, write **sat, hat, fin**

a. You're going to write the word (pause) **sat.** Say the sounds in **sat.** Get ready. (Tap for each sound as the children say:) *sss* (pause) *aaa* (pause) *t.*
• (Repeat until firm.)
b. Everybody, write the word (pause) **sat.** ✔
c. (Repeat steps *a* and *b* for **hat** and **fin.**)

EXERCISE 5

Write **that, this, sit**

a. You're going to write the word (pause) **that.** Think about the sounds in **that** and write the word. ✔
b. (Repeat step *a* for **this** and **sit.**)

LESSON 19

SOUND WRITING
EXERCISE 1

Write **e, a, m, b**

a. You're going to write some sounds.
b. Here's the first sound you're going to write. Listen. **eee.** What sound? (Signal.) *eee.*
c. Write **eee.** ✔
d. Next sound. Listen. **aaa.** What sound? (Signal.) *aaa.*
e. Write **aaa.** ✔
f. (Repeat steps *d* and *e* for **m** and **b.**)

EXERCISE 2

Write **ar**

a. Everybody, you're going to write the letters that go together and make the sound **are.** What sound? (Signal.) *Are.*
b. Write **ar.** ✔

WORD WRITING
EXERCISE 3

Write sound combination words **far, bar, farm, barn**

a. (Write on the board: **far, bar, farm, barn.**)
b. (Point to **far.**) Everybody, read this word the fast way. Get ready. (Signal.) *Far.* Yes, **far.**
c. Everybody, say the sounds you write for the word (pause) **far.** Get ready. (Touch **f, ar** as the children say:) *fff* (pause) *ar.*
• (Repeat until firm.)
d. (Erase **far.**) Everybody, write the word (pause) **far.** ✔
e. (Repeat steps *b–d* for **bar, farm,** and **barn.**)

EXERCISE 4

Say the sounds, write **if, it, sit, that**

a. You're going to write the word (pause) **if.** Say the sounds in **if.** Get ready. (Tap for each sound as the children say:) *iii* (pause) *fff.*
• (Repeat until firm.)
b. Everybody, write the word (pause) **if.** ✔
c. (Repeat steps *a* and *b* for **it, sit,** and **that.**)

EXERCISE 5

Write **sat, hat, the**

a. You're going to write the word (pause) **sat.** Think about the sounds in **sat** and write the word. ✔
b. (Repeat step *a* for **hat** and **the.**)

LESSON 20

SOUND WRITING
EXERCISE 1

Write **e, n, i, d**

a. You're going to write some sounds.
b. Here's the first sound you're going to write. Listen. **eee.** What sound? (Signal.) *eee.*

c. Write **eee.** ✔
d. Next sound. Listen. **nnn.** What sound? (Signal.) *nnn.*
e. Write **nnn.** ✔
f. (Repeat steps *d* and *e* for **i** and **d.**)

EXERCISE 2

Write **ar**

a. Everybody, you're going to write the letters that go together and make the sound **are.** What sound? (Signal.) *Are.*
b. Write **ar.** ✔

WORD WRITING
EXERCISE 3

Write sound combination words **barn, car, arm, farm**

a. (Write on the board: **barn, car, arm, farm.**)
b. (Point to **barn.**) Everybody, read this word the fast way. Get ready. (Signal.) *Barn.* Yes, **barn.**
c. Everybody, say the sounds you write for the word (pause) **barn.** Get ready. (Touch **b, ar, n** as the children say:) *b* (pause) *ar* (pause) *nnn.*
• (Repeat until firm.)
d. (Erase **barn.**) Everybody, write the word (pause) **barn.** ✔
e. (Repeat steps *b–d* for **car, arm,** and **farm.**)

EXERCISE 4

Say the sounds, write **cat, him, them**

a. You're going to write the word (pause) **cat.** Say the sounds in **cat.** Get ready. (Tap for each sound as the children say:) *k* (pause) *aaa* (pause) *t.*
• (Repeat until firm.)
b. Everybody, write the word (pause) **cat.** ✔
c. (Repeat steps *a* and *b* for **him** and **them.**)

EXERCISE 5

Write **hat, ham, hit, sit, this**

a. You're going to write the word (pause) **hat.** Think about the sounds in **hat** and write the word. ✔

b. (Repeat step *a* for **ham, hit, sit,** and **this.**)

LESSON 21

SOUND WRITING
EXERCISE 1

Write **e, i, r, a**

a. You're going to write some sounds.
b. Here's the first sound you're going to write. Listen. **eee.** What sound? (Signal.) *eee.*
c. Write **eee.** ✔
d. Next sound. Listen. **iii.** What sound? (Signal.) *iii.*
e. Write **iii.** ✔
f. (Repeat steps *d* and *e* for **r** and **a.**)

WORD WRITING
EXERCISE 2

Listen, say the sounds, write **is, has**

a. You're going to write the word (pause) **is.** When you write the word **is,** you write these sounds: **iii** (pause) **sss.**
b. Say the sounds you write for (pause) **is.** Get ready. (Tap for each sound as the children say:) *iii* (pause) *sss.*
• (Repeat until firm.)
c. Everybody, write the word (pause) **is.** ✔
d. (Repeat steps *a–c* for **has.**)

EXERCISE 3

Say the sounds, write **if, farm, tar, bat**

a. You're going to write the word (pause) **if.** Say the sounds in **if.** Get ready. (Tap for each sound as the children say:) *iii* (pause) *fff.*
• (Repeat until firm.)
b. Everybody, write the word (pause) **if.** ✔
c. (Repeat steps *a* and *b* for **farm, tar,** and **bat.**)

EXERCISE 4

Write **arm, car, hat, me, we**

a. You're going to write the word (pause) **arm.** Think about the sounds in **arm** and write the word. ✔
b. (Repeat step *a* for **car, hat, me,** and **we.**)

SENTENCE WRITING
EXERCISE 5

Write one sentence

Children are not responsible for capital letters.

a. Listen to this sentence. **He is fat.** Say that sentence. Get ready. (Signal.) *He is fat.*
b. Now you're going to say that sentence the slow way. Get ready. (Signal.) (Signal for each word as the children say:) *He* (pause) *is* (pause) *fat.*
c. Everybody, write the sentence. Spell each word the right way. Remember to put a period at the end of your sentence. ✔

LESSON 22

SOUND WRITING
EXERCISE 1

Write **o, e, c, p**

a. You're going to write some sounds.
b. Here's the first sound you're going to write. Listen. **ooo.** What sound? (Signal.) *ooo.*
c. Write **ooo.** ✔
d. Next sound. Listen. **eee.** What sound? (Signal.) *eee.*
e. Write **eee.** ✔
f. (Repeat steps *d* and *e* for **c** and **p.**)

WORD WRITING
EXERCISE 2

Say the sounds, write **this, far, we, barn, is, has**

a. You're going to write the word (pause) **this.** Say the sounds in **this.** Get ready. (Tap for each sound as the children say:) *th* (pause) *iii* (pause) *sss.*
- (Repeat until firm.)

b. Everybody, write the word (pause) **this.** ✔

c. (Repeat steps *a* and *b* for **far, we, barn, is,** and **has.**)

EXERCISE 3

Write **hat, sit, tar, it, that, me, if**

a. You're going to write the word (pause) **hat.** Think about the sounds in **hat** and write the word. ✔

b. (Repeat step *a* for **sit, tar, it, that, me,** and **if.**)

SENTENCE WRITING
EXERCISE 4

Write one sentence

a. Listen to this sentence. **He is a man.** Say that sentence. Get ready. (Signal.) *He is a man.*

b. Now you're going to say that sentence the slow way. Get ready. (Signal for each word as the children say:) *He* (pause) *is* (pause) *a* (pause) *man.*

c. Everybody, write the sentence. Spell each word the right way. Remember to put a period at the end of your sentence. ✔

LESSON **23**

SOUND WRITING
EXERCISE 1

Write **o, b, m, n**

a. You're going to write some sounds.

b. Here's the first sound you're going to write. Listen. **ooo.** What sound? (Signal.) *ooo.*

c. Write **ooo.** ✔

d. Next sound. Listen. **b.** What sound? (Signal.) *b.*

e. Write **b.** ✔

f. (Repeat steps *d* and *e* for **m** and **n.**)

EXERCISE 2

Introduce sound combination **sh**

a. (Write on the board: **sh.**)

b. (Point to **sh.**) Everybody, tell me the sound these letters make. Get ready. (Signal.) *sh.* Yes, **sh.**

c. (Erase **sh.**) Everybody, write the letters that go together and make the sound **sh.** ✔

WORD WRITING
EXERCISE 3

Say the sounds, write **bad, him, arm, men, ten, set**

a. You're going to write the word (pause) **bad.** Say the sounds in **bad.** Get ready. (Tap for each sound as the children say:) *b* (pause) *aaa* (pause) *d.*
- (Repeat until firm.)

b. Everybody, write the word (pause) **bad.** ✔

c. (Repeat steps *a* and *b* for **him, arm, men, ten,** and **set.**)

EXERCISE 4

Write **met, bar, farm, sad, has**

a. You're going to write the word (pause) **met.** Think about the sounds in **met** and write the word. ✔

b. (Repeat step *a* for **bar, farm, sad,** and **has.**)

SENTENCE WRITING
EXERCISE 5

Write one sentence

a. Listen to this sentence. **He is a fat man.** Say that sentence. Get ready. (Signal.) *He is a fat man.*

b. Now you're going to say that sentence the slow way. Get ready. (Signal for each word as the children say:) *He* (pause) *is* (pause) *a* (pause) *fat* (pause) *man.*

c. Everybody, write the sentence. Spell each word the right way. Remember to put a period at the end of your sentence. ✔

LESSON 24

SOUND WRITING
EXERCISE 1

Write o, e, g, f

a. You're going to write some sounds.
b. Here's the first sound you're going to write. Listen. **ooo.** What sound? (Signal.) *ooo.*
c. Write **ooo.** ✔
d. Next sound. Listen. **eee.** What sound? (Signal.) *eee.*
e. Write **eee.** ✔
f. (Repeat steps *d* and *e* for **g** and **f.**)

EXERCISE 2

Introduce sound combination sh

a. (Write on the board: **sh.**)
b. (Point to **sh.**) Everybody, tell me the sound these letters make. Get ready. (Signal.) *sh.* Yes, **sh.**
c. (Erase **sh.**) Everybody, write the letters that go together and make the sound **sh.** ✔

WORD WRITING
EXERCISE 3

Write sound combination words she, wish, ship

a. (Write on the board: **she, wish, ship.**)
b. (Point to **she.**) Everybody, read this word the fast way. Get ready. (Signal.) *She.* Yes, **she.**

c. Everybody, say the sounds you write for the word (pause) **she.** Get ready. (Touch **sh, e** as the children say:) *sh* (pause) *ēēē.*
• (Repeat until firm.)
d. (Erase **she.**) Everybody, write the word (pause) **she.** ✔
e. (Repeat steps *b–d* for **wish** and **ship.**)

EXERCISE 4

Listen, say the sounds, write will

a. You're going to write the word (pause) **will.** When you write the word **will,** you write these sounds: **www** (pause) **iii** (pause) **lll** (pause) **lll.**
b. Say the sounds you write for (pause) **will.** Get ready. (Tap for each sound as the children say:) *www* (pause) *iii* (pause) *lll* (pause) *lll.*
• (Repeat until firm.)
c. Everybody, write the word (pause) **will.** ✔

EXERCISE 5

Say the sounds, write did, met, bet

a. You're going to write the word (pause) **did.** Say the sounds in **did.** Get ready. (Tap for each sound as the children say:) *d* (pause) *iii* (pause) *d.*
• (Repeat until firm.)
b. Everybody, write the word (pause) **did.** ✔
c. (Repeat steps *a* and *b* for **met** and **bet.**)

EXERCISE 6

Write is, has, that, ran, bad, me

a. You're going to write the word (pause) **is.** Think about the sounds in **is** and write the word. ✔
b. (Repeat step *a* for **has, that, ran, bad,** and **me.**)

SENTENCE WRITING
EXERCISE 7

Write one sentence

a. Listen to this sentence. **He has a cat.** Say that sentence. Get ready. (Signal.) *He has a cat.*

b. Now you're going to say that sentence the slow way. Get ready. (Signal for each word as the children say:)
He (pause) *has* (pause) *a* (pause) *cat.*

c. Everybody, write the sentence. Spell each word the right way. ✔

LESSON 25

SOUND WRITING
EXERCISE 1

Write **e, r, o, c, d, t**

a. You're going to write some sounds.

b. Here's the first sound you're going to write. Listen. **eee.** What sound? (Signal.) *eee.*

c. Write **eee.** ✔

d. Next sound. Listen. **rrr.** What sound? (Signal.) *rrr.*

e. Write **rrr.** ✔

f. (Repeat steps *d* and *e* for **o, c, d,** and **t.**)

EXERCISE 2

Introduce sound combination **sh**

a. (Write on the board: **sh.**)

b. (Point to **sh.**) Everybody, tell me the sound these letters make. Get ready. (Signal.) *sh.* Yes, **sh.**

c. (Erase **sh.**) Everybody, write the letters that go together and make the sound **sh.** ✔

WORD WRITING
EXERCISE 3

Write sound combination words **ship, she, wish, fish**

a. (Write on the board: **ship, she, wish, fish.**)

b. (Point to **ship.**) Everybody, read this word the fast way. Get ready. (Signal.) *Ship.* Yes, **ship.**

c. Everybody, say the sounds you write for the word (pause) **ship.** Get ready. (Touch **sh, i, p** as the children say:)
sh (pause) *iii* (pause) *p.*

• (Repeat until firm.)

d. (Erase **ship.**) Everybody, write the word (pause) **ship.** ✔

e. (Repeat steps *b–d* for **she, wish,** and **fish.**)

EXERCISE 4

Listen, say the sounds, write **was, will**

a. You're going to write the word (pause) **was.** When you write the word **was,** you write these sounds:
www (pause) **aaa** (pause) **sss.**

b. Say the sounds you write for (pause) **was.** Get ready. (Tap for each sound as the children say:)
www (pause) *aaa* (pause) *sss.*

• (Repeat until firm.)

c. Everybody, write the word (pause) **was.** ✔

d. (Repeat step *a–c* for **will.**)

EXERCISE 5

Say the sounds, write **this, him, far**

a. You're going to write the word (pause) **this.** Say the sounds in **this.** Get ready. (Tap for each sound as the children say:)
th (pause) *iii* (pause) *sss.*

• (Repeat until firm.)

b. Everybody, write the word (pause) **this.** ✔

c. (Repeat steps *a* and *b* for **him** and **far.**)

EXERCISE 6

Write **did, hat, men**

a. You're going to write the word (pause) **did.** Think about the sounds in **did** and write the word. ✔

b. (Repeat step *a* for **hat** and **men.**)

SENTENCE WRITING
EXERCISE 7

Write one sentence

a. Listen to this sentence. **He has a sad rat.** Say that sentence. Get ready. (Signal.) *He has a sad rat.*

b. Now you're going to say that sentence the slow way. Get ready. (Signal for each word as the children say:) *He* (pause) *has* (pause) *a* (pause) *sad* (pause) *rat.*

c. Everybody, write the sentence. Spell each word the right way. ✔

LESSON 26

SOUND WRITING
EXERCISE 1

Write **e, p, o, g, b, n**

a. You're going to write some sounds.

b. Here's the first sound you're going to write. Listen. **eee.** What sound? (Signal.) *eee.*

c. Write **eee.** ✔

d. Next sound. Listen. **p.** What sound? (Signal.) *p.*

e. Write **p.** ✔

f. (Repeat steps *d* and *e* for **o, g, b,** and **n.**)

EXERCISE 2

Write **sh**

a. Everybody, you're going to write the letters that go together and make the sound **sh.** What sound? (Signal.) *sh.*

b. Write **sh.** ✔

WORD WRITING
EXERCISE 3

Write sound combination words **she, fish, ship, dish**

a. (Write on the board: **she, fish, ship, dish.**)

b. (Point to **she.**) Everybody, read this word the fast way. Get ready. (Signal.) *She.* Yes, **she.**

c. Everybody, say the sounds you write for the word (pause) **she.** Get ready. (Touch **sh, e** as the children say:) *sh* (pause) *ēēē.*

• (Repeat until firm.)

d. (Erase **she.**) Everybody, write the word (pause) **she.** ✔

e. (Repeat steps *b–d* for **fish, ship,** and **dish.**)

EXERCISE 4

Say the sounds, write **was, cop, top**

a. You're going to write the word (pause) **was.** Say the sounds in **was.** Get ready. (Tap for each sound as the children say:) *www* (pause) *aaa* (pause) *sss.*

• (Repeat until firm.)

b. Everybody, write the word (pause) **was.** ✔

c. (Repeat steps *a* and *b* for **cop** and **top.**)

EXERCISE 5

Write **not, hot, barn, arm, then**

a. You're going to write the word (pause) **not.** Think about the sounds in **not** and write the word. ✔

b. (Repeat step *a* for **hot, barn, arm,** and **then.**)

SENTENCE WRITING
EXERCISE 6

Write one sentence

a. Listen to this sentence. **She has a ram.** Say that sentence. Get ready. (Signal.) *She has a ram.*

b. Now you're going to say that sentence the slow way. Get ready. (Signal for each word as the children say:) *She* (pause) *has* (pause) *a* (pause) *ram.*

c. Everybody, write the sentence. Spell each word the right way. ✔

LESSON 27

SOUND WRITING
EXERCISE 1

Write **i, r, o, c, g, w**

a. You're going to write some sounds.

b. Here's the first sound you're going to write. Listen. **iii.** What sound? (Signal.) *iii.*

c. Write **iii.** ✔

d. Next sound. Listen **rrr.** What sound? (Signal.) *rrr.*

e. Write **rrr.** ✔

f. (Repeat steps *d* and *e* for **o, c, g,** and **w.**)

EXERCISE 2

Write **sh**

a. Everybody, you're going to write the letters that go together and make the sound **sh.** What sound? (Signal.) *sh.*

b. Write **sh.** ✔

WORD WRITING
EXERCISE 3

Write sound combination words **dish, ship, shop**

a. (Write on the board: **dish, ship, shop.**)

b. (Point to **dish.**) Everybody, read this word the fast way. Get ready. (Signal.) *Dish.* Yes, **dish.**

c. Everybody, say the sounds you write for the word (pause) **dish.** Get ready. (Touch **d, i, sh** as the children say:) *d* (pause) *iii* (pause) *sh.*

• (Repeat until firm.)

d. (Erase **dish.**) Everybody, write the word (pause) **dish.** ✔

e. (Repeat steps *b–d* for **ship** and **shop.**)

EXERCISE 4

Say the sounds, write **car, was, has, is**

a. You're going to write the word (pause) **car.** Say the sounds in **car.** Get ready. (Tap for each sound as the children say:) *k* (pause) *ar.*

• (Repeat until firm.)

b. Everybody, write the word (pause) **car.** ✔

c. (Repeat steps *a* and *b* for **was, has,** and **is.**)

EXERCISE 5

Write **we, he, not, hop, far, did, this**

a. You're going to write the word (pause) **we.** Think about the sounds in **we** and write the word. ✔

b. (Repeat step *a* for **he, not, hop, far, did,** and **this.**)

SENTENCE WRITING
EXERCISE 6

Write one sentence

a. Listen to this sentence. **That cop has fish.** Say that sentence. Get ready. (Signal.) *That cop has fish.*

b. Now you're going to say that sentence the slow way. Get ready. (Signal for each word as the children say:) *That* (pause) *cop* (pause) *has* (pause) *fish.*

c. Everybody, write the sentence. Spell each word the right way. ✔

LESSON 28

SOUND WRITING
EXERCISE 1

Write **e, n, m, c, p, l**

a. You're going to write some sounds.

b. Here's the first sound you're going to write. Listen. **eee.** What sound? (Signal.) *eee.*

c. Write **eee.** ✔

d. Next sound. Listen. **nnn.** What sound? (Signal.) *nnn.*

e. Write **nnn.** ✔

f. (Repeat steps *d* and *e* for **m, c, p,** and **l.**)

EXERCISE 2

Write **ar, th, sh**

a. Everybody, you're going to write the two letters that go together and make the sound **ar.** What sound? (Signal.) *Are.*

b. Write **ar.** ✔

c. (Repeat steps *a* and *b* for **th** and **sh.**)

WORD WRITING
EXERCISE 3

Say the sounds, write **shop, barn, wet, dish, will**

a. You're going to write the word (pause) **shop.** Say the sounds in **shop.** Get ready. (Tap for each sound as the children say:) *sh* (pause) *ooo* (pause) *p.*
• (Repeat until firm.)
b. Everybody, write the word (pause) **shop.** ✔
c. (Repeat steps *a* and *b* for **barn, wet, dish,** and **will.**)

EXERCISE 4

Write **ten, met, fat, was, is, that, hat, hop, cop**

a. You're going to write the word (pause) **ten.** Think about the sounds in **ten** and write the word. ✔
b. (Repeat step *a* for **met, fat, was, is, that, hat, hop,** and **cop.**)

SENTENCE WRITING
EXERCISE 5

Write one sentence

a. Listen to this sentence. **She is not sad.** Say that sentence. Get ready. (Signal.) *She is not sad.*
b. Now you're going to say that sentence the slow way. Get ready. (Signal for each word as the children say:) *She* (pause) *is* (pause) *not* (pause) *sad.*
c. Everybody, write the sentence. Spell each word the right way. ✔

LESSON 29

SOUND WRITING
EXERCISE 1

Write **o, r, f, g**

a. You're going to write some sounds.
b. Here's the first sound you're going to write. Listen. **ooo.** What sound? (Signal.) *ooo.*

c. Write **ooo.** ✔
d. Next sound. Listen. **rrr.** What sound? (Signal.) *rrr.*
e. Write **rrr.** ✔
f. (Repeat steps *d* and *e* for **f** and **g.**)

EXERCISE 2

Write **th, ar, sh**

a. Everybody, you're going to write the letters that go together and make the sound **th.** What sound? (Signal.) *th.*
b. Write **th.** ✔
c. (Repeat steps *a* and *b* for **ar** and **sh.**)

WORD WRITING
EXERCISE 3

Listen, say the sounds, write **his**

a. You're going to write the word (pause) **his.** When you write the word **his,** you write these sounds: *h* (pause) *iii* (pause) *sss.*
b. Say the sounds you write for (pause) **his.** Get ready. (Tap for each sound as the children say:) *h* (pause) *iii* (pause) *sss.*
• (Repeat until firm.)
c. Everybody, write the word (pause) **his.** ✔

EXERCISE 4

Say the sounds, write **ship, wish, farm, him, then**

a. You're going to write the word (pause) **ship.** Say the sounds in **ship.** Get ready. (Tap for each sound as the children say:) *sh* (pause) *iii* (pause) *p.*
• (Repeat until firm.)
b. Everybody, write the word (pause) **ship.** ✔
c. (Repeat steps *a* and *b* for **wish, farm, him,** and **then.**)

EXERCISE 5

Write **bet, wet, that, arm, cop, hop, shop**

a. You're going to write the word (pause) **bet.** Think about the sounds in **bet** and write the word. ✔

b. (Repeat step *a* for **wet, that, arm, cop, hop,** and **shop.**)

SENTENCE WRITING
EXERCISE 6

Write one sentence

a. Listen to this sentence. **She did not shop.** Say that sentence. Get ready. (Signal.) *She did not shop.*

b. Now you're going to say that sentence the slow way. Get ready. (Signal for each word as the children say:) *She* (pause) *did* (pause) *not* (pause) *shop.*

c. Everybody, write the sentence. Spell each word the right way. ✔

LESSON 30

SOUND WRITING
EXERCISE 1

Write **e, u, d, t**

a. You're going to write some sounds.

b. Here's the first sound you're going to write. Listen. **eee.** What sound? (Signal.) *eee.*

c. Write **eee.** ✔

d. Next sound. Listen. **uuu.** What sound? (Signal.) *uuu.*

e. Write **uuu.** ✔

f. (Repeat steps *d* and *e* for **d** and **t.**)

EXERCISE 2

Write **sh, ar, th**

a. Everybody, you're going to write the letters that go together and make the sound **sh.** What sound? (Signal.) *sh.*

b. Write **sh.** ✔

c. (Repeat steps *a* and *b* for **ar** and **th.**)

WORD WRITING
EXERCISE 3

Say the sounds, write **is, his, if, tar, them, set**

a. You're going to write the word (pause) **is.** Say the sounds in **is.** Get ready. (Tap for each sound as the children say:) *iii* (pause) *sss.*

• (Repeat until firm.)

b. Everybody, write the word (pause) **is.** ✔

c. (Repeat steps *a* and *b* for **his, if, tar, them,** and **set.**)

EXERCISE 4

Write **bar, was, hot, met, this**

a. You're going to write the word (pause) **bar.** Think about the sounds in **bar** and write the word. ✔

b. (Repeat step *a* for **was, hot, met,** and **this.**)

SENTENCE WRITING
EXERCISE 5

Write one sentence

a. Listen to this sentence. **We did not shop.** Say that sentence. Get ready. (Signal.) *We did not shop.*

b. Now you're going to say that sentence the slow way. Get ready. (Signal for each word as the children say:) *We* (pause) *did* (pause) *not* (pause) *shop.*

c. Everybody, write the sentence. Spell each word the right way. ✔

LESSON 31

SOUND WRITING
EXERCISE 1

Write **u, o, b, m**

a. You're going to write some sounds.

b. Here's the first sound you're going to write. Listen. **uuu.** What sound? (Signal.) *uuu.*

c. Write **uuu.** ✔

d. Next sound. Listen. **ooo.** What sound?
(Signal.) *ooo.*

e. Write **ooo.** ✔

f. (Repeat steps *d* and *e* for **b** and **m.**)

EXERCISE 2

Introduce sound combination ing

a. (Write on the board: **ing.**)

b. (Point to **ing.**) Everybody, tell me the
sound these letters make. Get ready.
(Signal.) *ing.* Yes, **ing.**

c. (Erase **ing.**) Everybody, write the letters
that go together and make the sound
ing. ✔

WORD WRITING
EXERCISE 3

Say the sounds, write has, his, mop,
mat, went, wish

a. You're going to write the word (pause)
has. Say the sounds in **has.** Get ready.
(Tap for each sound as the children say:)
h (pause) *aaa* (pause) *sss.*

• (Repeat until firm.)

b. Everybody, write the word (pause) **has.** ✔

c. (Repeat steps a and b for **his, mop,
mat, went,** and **wish.**)

EXERCISE 4

Write far, barn, we, it, then, bad

a. You're going to write the word (pause)
far. Think about the sounds in **far** and
write the word. ✔

b. (Repeat step *a* for **barn, we, it, then,**
and **bad.**)

SENTENCE WRITING
EXERCISE 5

Write one sentence

a. Listen to this sentence. **That dish was
hot.** Say that sentence. Get ready.
(Signal.) *That dish was hot.*

b. Now you're going to say that sentence
the slow way. Get ready. (Signal for each
word as the children say:) *That* (pause)
dish (pause) *was* (pause) *hot.*

c. Everybody, write the sentence. Spell
each word the right way. ✔

LESSON 32

SOUND WRITING
EXERCISE 1

Write u, n, e, c

a. You're going to write some sounds.

b. Here's the first sound you're going to
write. Listen. **uuu.** What sound?
(Signal.) *uuu.*

c. Write **uuu.** ✔

d. Next sound. Listen. **nnn.** What sound?
(Signal.) *nnn.*

e. Write **nnn.** ✔

f. (Repeat steps *d* and *e* for **e** and **c.**)

EXERCISE 2

Introduce sound combination ing

a. (Write on the board: **ing.**)

b. (Point to **ing.**) Everybody, tell me the
sound these letters make. Get ready.
(Signal.) *ing.* Yes, **ing.**

c. (Erase **ing.**) Everybody, write the letters
that go together and make the sound
ing. ✔

WORD WRITING
EXERCISE 3

Write sound combination words ring,
sing, thing

a. (Write on the board: **ring, sing, thing.**)

b. (Point to **ring.**) Everybody, read this
word the fast way. Get ready. (Signal.)
Ring. Yes, **ring.**

c. Everybody, say the sounds you write
for the word (pause) **ring.** Get ready.
(Touch **r, ing** as the children say:)
rrr (pause) *ing.*

• (Repeat until firm.)

d. (Erase **ring.**) Everybody, write the word
(pause) **ring.** ✔

e. (Repeat steps *b–d* for **sing** and **thing.**)

23

EXERCISE 4

Say the sounds, write cow, how, now, went

a. You're going to write the word (pause) **cow.** Say the sounds in **cow.** Get ready. (Tap for each sound as the children say:) *k* (pause) *ooo* (pause) *www.*
* (Repeat until firm.)
b. Everybody, write the word (pause) **cow. ✔**
c. (Repeat steps *a* and *b* for **how, now, and went.**)

EXERCISE 5

Write car, farm, if, him, ship

a. You're going to write the word (pause) **car.** Think about the sounds in **car** and write the word. ✔
b. (Repeat step *a* for **farm, if, him,** and **ship.**)

SENTENCE WRITING
EXERCISE 6

Write one sentence

a. Listen to this sentence. **A fish was in a dish.** Say that sentence. Get ready. (Signal.) *A fish was in a dish.*
b. Now you're going to say that sentence the slow way. Get ready. (Signal for each word as the children say:) *A* (pause) *fish* (pause) *was* (pause) *in* (pause) *a* (pause) *dish.*
c. Everybody, write the sentence. Spell each word the right way. ✔

LESSON 33

SOUND WRITING
EXERCISE 1

Write e, d, o, t

a. You're going to write some sounds.
b. Here's the first sound you're going to write. Listen. **eee.** What sound? (Signal.) *eee.*
c. Write **eee. ✔**

d. Next sound. Listen. **d.** What sound? (Signal.) *d.*
e. Write **d. ✔**
f. (Repeat steps *d* and *e* for **o** and **t.**)

EXERCISE 2

Write ing

a. Everybody, you're going to write the letters that go together and make the sound **ing.** What sound? (Signal.) *ing.*
b. Write **ing. ✔**

WORD WRITING
EXERCISE 3

Write sound combination words sing, thing, ring

a. (Write on the board: **sing, thing, ring.**)
b. (Point to **sing.**) Everybody, read this word the fast way. Get ready. (Signal.) *Sing.* Yes, **sing.**
c. Everybody, say the sounds you write for the word (pause) **sing.** Get ready. (Touch **s, ing** as the children say:) *sss* (pause) *ing.*
* (Repeat until firm.)
d. (Erase **sing.**) Everybody, write the word (pause) **sing. ✔**
e. (Repeat steps *b–d* for **thing** and **ring.**)

EXERCISE 4

Listen, say the sounds, write on

a. You're going to write the word (pause) **on.** When you write the word **on,** you write these sounds: **ooo** (pause) **nnn.**
b. Say the sounds you write for (pause) **on.** Get ready. (Tap for each sound as the children say:) *ooo* (pause) *nnn.*
* (Repeat until firm.)
c. Everybody, write the word (pause) **on. ✔**

EXERCISE 5

Say the sounds, write hen, went, dug, bug, run, sun

a. You're going to write the word (pause) **hen.** Say the sounds in **hen.** Get ready. (Tap for each sound as the children say:) *h* (pause) *eee* (pause) *nnn.*

24

- (Repeat until firm.)
b. Everybody, write the word (pause) **hen.** ✔
c. (Repeat steps *a* and *b* for **went, dug, bug, run,** and **sun.**)

EXERCISE 6

Write **how, will, has**

a. You're going to write the word (pause) **how.** Think about the sounds in **how** and write the word. ✔
b. (Repeat step *a* for **will** and **has.**)

SENTENCE WRITING
EXERCISE 7

Write one sentence

a. Listen to this sentence. **The cow was in the barn.** Say that sentence. Get ready. (Signal.) *The cow was in the barn.*
b. Now you're going to say that sentence the slow way. Get ready. (Signal for each word as the children say:)
The (pause) *cow* (pause) *was* (pause) *in* (pause) *the* (pause) *barn.*
c. Everybody, write the sentence. Spell each word the right way. ✔

LESSON 34

SOUND WRITING
EXERCISE 1

Write **u, o, g, b**

a. You're going to write some sounds.
b. Here's the first sound you're going to write. Listen. **uuu.** What sound? (Signal.) *uuu.*
c. Write **uuu.** ✔
d. Next sound. Listen. **ooo.** What sound? (Signal.) *ooo.*
e. Write **ooo.** ✔
f. (Repeat steps *d* and *e* for **g** and **b.**)

WORD WRITING
EXERCISE 2

Say the sounds, write **thing, shop, park**

a. You're going to write the word (pause) **thing.** Say the sounds in **thing.** Get ready. (Tap for each sound as the children say:) *th* (pause) *ing.*
- (Repeat until firm.)
b. Everybody, write the word (pause) **thing.** ✔
c. (Repeat steps *a* and *b* for **shop** and **park.**)

EXERCISE 3

Write **cop, wish, far, ring, rug, fun, bug, now, how**

a. You're going to write the word (pause) **cop.** Think about the sounds in **cop** and write the word. ✔
b. (Repeat step *a* for **wish, far, ring, rug, fun, bug, now,** and **how.**)

SENTENCE WRITING
EXERCISE 4

Write one sentence

a. Listen to this sentence. **A hen was on a farm.** Say that sentence. Get ready. (Signal.) *A hen was on a farm.*
b. Now you're going to say that sentence the slow way. Get ready. (Signal for each word as the children say:) *A* (pause) *hen* (pause) *was* (pause) *on* (pause) *a* (pause) *farm.*
c. Everybody, write the sentence. Spell each word the right way. ✔

LESSON 35

SOUND WRITING
EXERCISE 1

Write **u, o, p, f**

a. You're going to write some sounds.
b. Here's the first sound you're going to write. Listen. **uuu.** What sound? (Signal.) *uuu.*
c. Write **uuu.** ✔

d. Next sound. Listen. **ooo.** What sound? (Signal.) *ooo.*

e. Write **ooo.** ✔

f. (Repeat steps *d* and *e* for **p** and **f.**)

WORD WRITING
EXERCISE 2

Listen, say the sounds, write **to, do**

a. You're going to write the word (pause) **to.** When you write the word **to,** you write these sounds: **t** (pause) **ooo.**

b. Say the sounds you write for (pause) **to.** Get ready. (Tap for each sound as the children say:) *t* (pause) *ooo.*

• (Repeat until firm.)

c. Everybody, write the word (pause) **to.** ✔

d. (Repeat steps *a–c* for **do.**)

EXERCISE 3

Say the sounds, write **if, cow, dark, sing**

a. You're going to write the word (pause) **if.** Say the sounds in **if.** Get ready. (Tap for each sound as the children say:) *iii* (pause) *fff.*

• (Repeat until firm.)

b. Everybody, write the word (pause) **if.** ✔

c. (Repeat steps *a* and *b* for **cow, dark,** and **sing.**)

EXERCISE 4

Write **on, hen, then, now, dug, run, sun**

a. You're going to write the word (pause) **on.** Think about the sounds in **on** and write the word. ✔

b. (Repeat step *a* for **hen, then, now, dug, run,** and **sun.**)

SENTENCE WRITING
EXERCISE 5

Write one sentence

a. Listen to this sentence. **She was in the park.** Say that sentence. Get ready. (Signal.) *She was in the park.*

b. Now you're going to say that sentence the slow way. Get ready. (Signal for each word as the children say:) *She* (pause)

was (pause) *in* (pause) *the* (pause) *park.*

c. Everybody, write the sentence. Spell each word the right way. ✔

LESSON 36

WORD WRITING
EXERCISE 1

Say the sounds, write **to, do, bag, and, dig, ship, shop**

a. You're going to write the word (pause) **to.** Say the sounds in **to.** Get ready. (Tap for each sound as the children say:) *t* (pause) *ooo.*

• (Repeat until firm.)

b. Everybody, write the word (pause) **to.** ✔

c. (Repeat steps *a* and *b* for **do, bag, and, dig, ship,** and **shop.**)

EXERCISE 2

Write **far, thing, has, how**

a. You're going to write the word (pause) **far.** Think about the sounds in **far** and write the word. ✔

b. (Repeat step *a* for **thing, has,** and **how.**)

SENTENCE WRITING
EXERCISE 3

Write two sentences

a. Listen to this sentence. **The park was not dark.** Say that sentence. Get ready. (Signal.) *The park was not dark.*

b. Now you're going to say that sentence the slow way. Get ready. (Signal for each word as the children say:) *The* (pause) *park* (pause) *was* (pause) *not* (pause) *dark.*

c. Everybody, write the sentence. Spell each word the right way. ✔

d. (Repeat steps *a–c* for **He has a cat.**)

WORD WRITING
EXERCISE 1

Say the sounds, write **ring, dog, met, him**

a. You're going to write the word (pause) **ring.** Say the sounds in **ring.** Get ready. (Tap for each sound as the children say:) *rrr* (pause) *ing.*
- (Repeat until firm.)
b. Everybody, write the word (pause) **ring.** ✔
c. (Repeat steps *a* and *b* for **dog, met,** and **him.**)

EXERCISE 2

Write **went, that, bark, bug, cop, has, big, how**

a. You're going to write the word (pause) **went.** Think about the sounds in **went** and write the word. ✔
b. (Repeat step *a* for **that, bark, bug, cop, has, big,** and **how.**)

SENTENCE WRITING
EXERCISE 3

Write two sentences

a. Listen to this sentence. **His fish was not fat.** Say that sentence. Get ready. (Signal.) *His fish was not fat.*
b. Now you're going to say that sentence the slow way. Get ready. (Signal for each word as the children say:) *His* (pause) *fish* (pause) *was* (pause) *not* (pause) *fat.*
c. Everybody, write the sentence. Spell each word the right way. ✔
d. (Repeat steps *a–c* for **That cat is fat.**)

WORD WRITING
EXERCISE 1

Say the sounds, write **can, if, do, us, get, set**

a. You're going to write the word (pause) **can.** Say the sounds in **can.** Get ready. (Tap for each sound as the children say:) *k* (pause) *aaa* (pause) *nnn.*
- (Repeat until firm.)
b. Everybody, write the word (pause) **can.** ✔
c. (Repeat steps *a* and *b* for **if, do, us, get,** and **set.**)

EXERCISE 2

Write **to, has, sing, far, rug, ship, shop**

a. You're going to write the word (pause) **to.** Think about the sounds in **to** and write the word. ✔
b. (Repeat step *a* for **has, sing, far, rug, ship,** and **shop.**)

SENTENCE WRITING
EXERCISE 3

Write two sentences

a. Listen to this sentence. **His hat is not wet.** Say that sentence. Get ready. (Signal.) *His hat is not wet.*
b. Now you're going to say that sentence the slow way. Get ready. (Signal for each word as the children say:) *His* (pause) *hat* (pause) *is* (pause) *not* (pause) *wet.*
c. Everybody, write the sentence. Spell each word the right way. ✔
d. (Repeat *a–c* for **We will run and hop.**)

LESSON 39

WORD WRITING
EXERCISE 1

Listen, say the sounds, write **come**

a. You're going to write the word (pause) **come.** When you write the word **come,** you write these sounds: **k** (pause) **ooo** (pause) **mmm** (pause) **ēēē.**

b. Say the sounds you write for (pause) **come.** Get ready. (Tap for each sound as the children say:) *k* (pause) *ooo* (pause) *mmm* (pause) *ēēē.*

• (Repeat until firm.)

c. Everybody, write the word (pause) **come.** ✔

EXERCISE 2

Say the sounds, write **bag, bug, thing, with**

a. You're going to write the word (pause) **bag.** Say the sounds in **bag.** Get ready. (Tap for each sound as the children say:) *b* (pause) *aaa* (pause) *g.*

• (Repeat until firm.)

b. Everybody, write the word (pause) **bag.** ✔

c. (Repeat steps *a* and *b* for **bug, thing,** and **with.**)

EXERCISE 3

Write **sing, do, us, car, get, in**

a. You're going to write the word (pause) **sing.** Think about the sounds in **sing** and write the word. ✔

b. (Repeat step *a* for **do, us, car, get,** and **in.**)

SENTENCE WRITING
EXERCISE 4

Write two sentences

a. Listen to this sentence. **He has a cat and a rat.** Say that sentence. Get ready. (Signal.) *He has a cat and a rat.*

b. Now you're going to say that sentence the slow way. Get ready. (Signal for each word as the children say:)
He (pause) *has* (pause) *a* (pause) *cat* (pause) *and* (pause) *a* (pause) *rat.*

c. Everybody, write the sentence. Spell each word the right way. ✔

d. (Repeat *a–c* for **The cop was in the park.**)

LESSON 40

WORD WRITING
EXERCISE 1

Listen, say the sounds, write **come**

a. You're going to write the word (pause) **come.** When you write the word **come,** you write these sounds: **k** (pause) **ooo** (pause) **mmm** (pause) **ēēē.**

b. Say the sounds you write for (pause) **come.** Get ready. (Tap for each sound as the children say:) *k* (pause) *ooo* (pause) *mmm* (pause) *ēēē.*

• (Repeat until firm.)

c. Everybody, write the word (pause) **come.** ✔

EXERCISE 2

Say the sounds, write **how, cow, with**

a. You're going to write the word (pause) **how.** Say the sounds in **how.** Get ready. (Tap for each sound as the children say:) *h* (pause) *ooo* (pause) *www.*

• (Repeat until firm.)

b. Everybody, write the word (pause) **how.** ✔

c. (Repeat steps *a* and *b* for **cow** and **with.**)

EXERCISE 3

Listen, say the sounds, write **pill, hill**

a. You're going to write the word (pause) **pill.** When you write the word **pill,** you write these sounds: **p** (pause) **iii** (pause) **lll** (pause) **lll.**

b. Say the sounds you write for (pause) **pill.** Get ready. (Tap for each sound as the children say:) *p* (pause) *iii* (pause) *lll* (pause) *lll.*

• (Repeat until firm.)

c. Everybody, write the word (pause) **pill.** ✔

d. (Repeat steps *a–c* for **hill.**)

EXERCISE 4

Write **wish, barn, red, to, ring, has**

a. You're going to write the word (pause) **wish.** Think about the sounds in **wish** and write the word. ✔

b. (Repeat step *a* for **barn, red, to, ring,** and **has.**)

SENTENCE WRITING
EXERCISE 5

Write two sentences

a. Listen to this sentence. **She will hop and sing.** Say that sentence. Get ready. (Signal.) *She will hop and sing.*

b. Now you're going to say that sentence the slow way. Get ready. (Signal for each word as the children say:) *She* (pause) *will* (pause) *hop* (pause) *and* (pause) *sing.*

c. Everybody, write the sentence. Spell each word the right way. ✔

d. (Repeat steps *a–c* for **A bug was on a rug.**)

WORD WRITING
EXERCISE 1

Say the sounds, write **cup, us, come, swim, bed, get**

a. You're going to write the word (pause) **cup.** Say the sounds in **cup.** Get ready. (Tap for each sound as the children say:) *k* (pause) *uuu* (pause) *p.*

• (Repeat until firm.)

b. Everybody, write the word (pause) **cup.** ✔

c. (Repeat steps *a* and *b* for **us, come, swim, bed,** and **get.**)

EXERCISE 2

Write **dish, with, hill, arm**

a. You're going to write the word (pause) **dish.** Think about the sounds in **dish** and write the word. ✔

b. (Repeat step *a* for **with, hill,** and **arm.**)

SENTENCE WRITING
EXERCISE 3

Write two sentences

a. Listen to this sentence. **The cat was in the car.** Say that sentence. Get ready. (Signal.) *The cat was in the car.*

b. Now you're going to say that sentence the slow way. Get ready. (Signal for each word as the children say:) *The* (pause) *cat* (pause) *was* (pause) *in* (pause) *the* (pause) *car.*

c. Everybody, write the sentence. Spell each word the right way. ✔

d. (Repeat steps *a–c* for **That fan is not wet.**)

WORD WRITING
EXERCISE 1

Say the sounds, write **us, bus, top, stop, fed**

a. You're going to write the word (pause) **us.** Say the sounds in **us.** Get ready. (Tap for each sound as the children say:) *uuu* (pause) *sss.*

• (Repeat until firm.)

b. Everybody, write the word (pause) **us.** ✔

c. (Repeat steps *a* and *b* for **bus, top, stop,** and **fed.**)

EXERCISE 2

Write **bed, swim, if, come, wish, me, has**

a. You're going to write the word (pause) **bed.** Think about the sounds in **bed** and write the word. ✔

b. (Repeat step *a* for **swim, if, come, wish, me,** and **has.**)

SENTENCE WRITING
EXERCISE 3

Write two sentences

a. Listen to this sentence. **The rat was on the ship.** Say that sentence. Get ready. (Signal.) *The rat was on the ship.*

b. Now you're going to say that sentence the slow way. Get ready. (Signal for each word as the children say:)
The (pause) *rat* (pause) *was* (pause) *on* (pause) *the* (pause) *ship.*

c. Everybody, write the sentence. Spell each word the right way. ✔

d. (Repeat steps *a–c* for **A dog will run and bark.**)

LESSON 43

WORD WRITING
EXERCISE 1

Say the sounds, write **big, pit, ring, sing, dark**

a. You're going to write the word (pause) **big.** Say the sounds in **big.** Get ready. (Tap for each sound as the children say:)
b (pause) *iii* (pause) *g.*

• (Repeat until firm.)

b. Everybody, write the word (pause) **big.** ✔

c. (Repeat steps *a* and *b* for **pit, ring, sing,** and **dark.**)

EXERCISE 2

Write **mop, cop, us, fed, them**

a. You're going to write the word (pause) **mop.** Think about the sounds in **mop** and write the word. ✔

b. (Repeat step *a* for **cop, us, fed,** and **them.**)

SENTENCE WRITING
EXERCISE 3

Write two sentences

a. Listen to this sentence. **This fish will swim.** Say that sentence. Get ready. (Signal.) *This fish will swim.*

b. Now you're going to say that sentence the slow way. Get ready. (Signal for each word as the children say:)
This (pause) *fish* (pause) *will* (pause) *swim.*

c. Everybody, write the sentence. Spell each word the right way. ✔

d. (Repeat steps *a–c* for **She did not hit me.**)

LESSON 44

WORD WRITING
EXERCISE 1

Listen, say the sounds, write **said**

a. You're going to write the word (pause) **said.** When you write the word **said,** you write these sounds:
sss (pause) **aaa** (pause) **iii** (pause) **d.**

b. Say the sounds you write for (pause) **said.** Get ready. (Tap for each sound as the children say:)
sss (pause) *aaa* (pause) *iii* (pause) *d.*

• (Repeat until firm.)

c. Everybody, write the word (pause) **said.** ✔

EXERCISE 2

Say the sounds, write **come, him, then, went, to**

a. You're going to write the word (pause) **come.** Say the sounds in **come.** Get ready. (Tap for each sound as the children say:) *k* (pause) *ooo* (pause) *mmm* (pause) *ēēē.*

• (Repeat until firm.)

b. Everybody, write the word (pause) **come.** ✔

c. (Repeat steps *a* and *b* for **him, then, went,** and **to.**)

EXERCISE 3

Write **has, thing, with, get, us, hop**

a. You're going to write the word (pause) **has.** Think about the sounds in **has** and write the word. ✔

b. (Repeat step *a* for **thing, with, get, us,** and **hop.**)

SENTENCE WRITING
EXERCISE 4

Write two sentences

a. Listen to this sentence. **That man did not run.** Say that sentence. Get ready. (Signal.) *That man did not run.*

b. Now you're going to say that sentence the slow way. Get ready. (Signal for each word as the children say:) *That* (pause) *man* (pause) *did* (pause) *not* (pause) *run.*

c. Everybody, write the sentence. Spell each word the right way. ✔

d. (Repeat steps *a–c* for **This park is not big.**)

LESSON **45**

WORD WRITING
EXERCISE 1

Listen, say the sounds, write **said, bell, fell, tell**

a. You're going to write the word (pause) **said.** When you write the word **said,** you write these sounds: **sss** (pause) **aaa** (pause) **iii** (pause) **d.**

b. Say the sounds you write for (pause) **said.** Get ready. (Tap for each sound as the children say:) *sss* (pause) *aaa* (pause) *iii* (pause) *d.*

• (Repeat until firm.)

c. Everybody, write the word (pause) **said.** ✔

d. (Repeat steps *a–c* for **bell, fell,** and **tell.**)

EXERCISE 2

Say the sounds, write **come, tar, if**

a. You're going to write the word (pause) **come.** Say the sounds in **come.** Get ready. (Tap for each sound as the children say:) *k* (pause) *ooo* (pause) *mmm* (pause) *ēēē.*

• (Repeat until firm.)

b. Everybody, write the word (pause) **come.** ✔

c. (Repeat steps *a* and *b* for **tar** and **if.**)

EXERCISE 3

Write **us, bus, with, hill, ring**

a. You're going to write the word (pause) **us.** Think about the sounds in **us** and write the word. ✔

b. (Repeat step *a* for **bus, with, hill,** and **ring.**)

SENTENCE WRITING
EXERCISE 4

Write two sentences

a. Listen to this sentence. **That cow did not sing.** Say that sentence. Get ready. (Signal.) *That cow did not sing.*

b. Now you're going to say that sentence the slow way. Get ready. (Signal for each word as the children say:) *That* (pause) *cow* (pause) *did* (pause) *not* (pause) *sing.*

c. Everybody, write the sentence. Spell each word the right way. ✔

d. (Repeat steps *a–c* for **This bug will run and hop.**)

WORD WRITING
EXERCISE 1

Say the sounds, write **sell, tell, bell, said**

a. You're going to write the word (pause) **sell.** Say the sounds in **sell.** Get ready. (Tap for each sound as the children say:) *sss* (pause) *eee* (pause) *lll* (pause) *lll.*

• (Repeat until firm.)

b. Everybody, write the word (pause) **sell.** ✔

c. (Repeat steps *a* and *b* for **tell, bell,** and **said.**)

EXERCISE 2

Write **bet, ten, bug, mud, now, hit, swim**

a. You're going to write the word (pause) **bet.** Think about the sounds in **bet** and write the word. ✔

b. (Repeat step *a* for **ten, bug, mud, now, hit,** and **swim.**)

SENTENCE WRITING
EXERCISE 3

Write two sentences

a. Listen to this sentence. **We went to the farm.** Say that sentence. Get ready. (Signal.) *We went to the farm.*

b. Now you're going to say that sentence the slow way. Get ready. (Signal for each word as the children say:) *We* (pause) *went* (pause) *to* (pause) *the* (pause) *farm.*

c. Everybody, write the sentence. Spell each word the right way. ✔

d. (Repeat steps *a–c* for **She will come with me.**)

WORD WRITING
EXERCISE 1

Say the sounds, write **bell, fell, sell, thing, me, she**

a. You're going to write the word (pause) **bell.** Say the sounds in **bell.** Get ready. (Tap for each sound as the children say:) *b* (pause) *eee* (pause) *lll* (pause) *lll.*

• (Repeat until firm.)

b. Everybody, write the word (pause) **bell.** ✔

c. (Repeat steps *a* and *b* for **fell, sell, thing, me,** and **she.**)

EXERCISE 2

Write **do, said, them, come, hill, mad**

a. You're going to write the word (pause) **do.** Think about the sounds in **do** and write the word. ✔

b. (Repeat step *a* for **said, them, come, hill,** and **mad.**)

SENTENCE WRITING
EXERCISE 3

Write two sentences

a. Listen to this sentence. **The dog went to the barn.** Say that sentence. Get ready. (Signal.) *The dog went to the barn.*

b. Now you're going to say that sentence the slow way. Get ready. (Signal for each word as the children say:) *The* (pause) *dog* (pause) *went* (pause) *to* (pause) *the* (pause) *barn.*

c. Everybody, write the sentence. Spell each word the right way. ✔

d. (Repeat steps *a–c* for **A cow will run with us.**)

LESSON 48

WORD WRITING
EXERCISE 1

Say the sounds, write **dish, wish, fish, if, bark, sand**

- **a.** You're going to write the word (pause) **dish.** Say the sounds in **dish.** Get ready. (Tap for each sound as the children say:) *d* (pause) *iii* (pause) *sh.*
- • (Repeat until firm.)
- **b.** Everybody, write the word (pause) **dish.** ✔
- **c.** (Repeat steps *a* and *b* for **wish, fish, if, bark,** and **sand.**)

EXERCISE 2

Write **well, tell, said, his, has**

- **a.** You're going to write the word (pause) **well.** Think about the sounds in **well** and write the word. ✔
- **b.** (Repeat step *a* for **tell, said, his,** and **has.**)

SENTENCE WRITING
EXERCISE 3

Write two sentences

- **a.** Listen to this sentence. **He will come with us.** Say that sentence. Get ready. (Signal.) *He will come with us.*
- **b.** Now you're going to say that sentence the slow way. Get ready. (Signal for each word as the children say:) *He* (pause) *will* (pause) *come* (pause) *with* (pause) *us.*
- **c.** Everybody, write the sentence. Spell each word the right way. ✔
- **d.** (Repeat steps *a–c* for **That cop was mad.**)

LESSON 49

WORD WRITING
EXERCISE 1

Say the sounds, write **cup, up, us, bell, ship, cow**

- **a.** You're going to write the word (pause) **cup.** Say the sounds in **cup.** Get ready. (Tap for each sound as the children say:) *k* (pause) *uuu* (pause) *p.*
- • (Repeat until firm.)
- **b.** Everybody, write the word (pause) **cup.** ✔
- **c.** (Repeat steps *a* and *b* for **up, us, bell, ship,** and **cow.**)

EXERCISE 2

Write **to, went, car, fell, sing, how**

- **a.** You're going to write the word (pause) **to.** Think about the sounds in **to** and write the word. ✔
- **b.** (Repeat step *a* for **went, car, fell, sing,** and **how.**)

SENTENCE WRITING
EXERCISE 3

Write two sentences

- **a.** Listen to this sentence. **That dish was in the mud.** Say that sentence. Get ready. (Signal.) *That dish was in the mud.*
- **b.** Now you're going to say that sentence the slow way. Get ready. (Signal for each word as the children say:) *That* (pause) *dish* (pause) *was* (pause) *in* (pause) *the* (pause) *mud.*
- **c.** Everybody, write the sentence. Spell each word the right way. ✔
- **d.** (Repeat steps *a–c* for **His dog will bark.**)

LESSON 50

SOUND WRITING
EXERCISE 1

Introduce sound combination **al**

a. (Write on the board: **al.**)
b. (Point to **al.**) Everybody, tell me the sound these letters make. Get ready. (Signal.) *All.* Yes, **all.**
c. (Erase **al.**) Everybody, write the two letters that go together and make the sound **all.** ✔

WORD WRITING
EXERCISE 2

Say the sounds, write **swim, ring, wet, hand**

a. You're going to write the word (pause) **swim.** Say the sounds in **swim.** Get ready. (Tap for each sound as the children say:) *sss* (pause) *www* (pause) *iii* (pause) *mmm.*
• (Repeat until firm.)
b. Everybody, write the word (pause) **swim.** ✔
c. (Repeat steps *a–b* for **ring, wet,** and **hand.**)

EXERCISE 3

Write **sand, it, hill, well, met, said**

a. You're going to write the word (pause) **sand.** Think about the sounds in **sand** and write the word. ✔
b. (Repeat step *a* for **it, hill, well, met,** and **said.**)

SENTENCE WRITING
EXERCISE 4

Write two sentences

a. Listen to this sentence. **The hen sat on the fan.** Say that sentence. Get ready. (Signal.) *The hen sat on the fan.*

b. Now you're going to say that sentence the slow way. Get ready. (Signal for each word as the children say:) *The* (pause) *hen* (pause) *sat* (pause) *on* (pause) *the* (pause) *fan.*
c. Everybody, write the sentence. Spell each word the right way. ✔
d. (Repeat steps *a–c* for **His cat ran in the park.**)

LESSON 51

SOUND WRITING
EXERCISE 1

Introduce sound combination **al**

a. (Write on the board: **al.**)
b. (Point to **al.**) Everybody, tell me the sound these letters make. Get ready. (Signal.) *All.* Yes, **all.**
c. (Erase **al.**) Everybody, write the two letters that go together and make the sound **all.** ✔

WORD WRITING
EXERCISE 2

Write sound combination words **all, ball, fall, also**

a. (Write on the board: **all, ball, fall, also.**)
b. (Point to **all.**) Everybody, read this word the fast way. Get ready. (Signal.) *All.* Yes, **all.**
c. Everybody, say the sounds you write for the word (pause) **all.** Get ready. (Touch **al, l** as the children say:) *al* (pause) *lll.*
• (Repeat until firm.)
d. (Erase **all.**) Everybody, write the word (pause) **all.** ✔
e. (Repeat steps *b–d* for **ball, fall,** and **also.**)

EXERCISE 3

Say the sounds, write **cap, pig, nut**

a. You're going to write the word (pause) **cap.** Say the sounds in **cap.** Get ready. (Tap for each sound as the children say:) *k* (pause) *aaa* (pause) *p.*

- (Repeat until firm.)
b. Everybody, write the word (pause) **cap.** ✔
c. (Repeat steps *a* and *b* for **pig** and **nut.**)

EXERCISE 4

Write **big, rug, bus, dark**

a. You're going to write the word (pause) **big.** Think about the sounds in **big** and write the word. ✔
b. (Repeat step *a* for **rug, bus,** and **dark.**)

SENTENCE WRITING
EXERCISE 5

Write two sentences

a. Listen to this sentence. **His dog can swim.** Say that sentence. Get ready. (Signal.) *His dog can swim.*
b. Now you're going to say that sentence the slow way. Get ready. (Signal for each word as the children say:) *His* (pause) *dog* (pause) *can* (pause) *swim.*
c. Everybody, write the sentence. Spell each word the right way. ✔
d. (Repeat steps *a–c* for **She will sell a hat.**)

LESSON 52

SOUND WRITING
EXERCISE 1

Introduce sound combination **al**

a. (Write on the board: **al.**)
b. (Point to **al.**) Everybody, tell me the sound these letters make. Get ready. (Signal.) *All.* Yes, **all.**
c. (Erase **al.**) Everybody, write the two letters that go together and make the sound **all.** ✔

WORD WRITING
EXERCISE 2

Write sound combination words **salt, call, fall**

a. (Write on the board: **salt, call, fall.**)

b. (Point to **salt.**) Everybody, read this word the fast way. Get ready. (Signal.) *Salt.* Yes, **salt.**
c. Everybody, say the sounds you write for the word (pause) **salt.** Get ready. (Touch **s, al, t** as the children say:) *sss* (pause) *al* (pause) *t.*
- (Repeat until firm.)
d. (Erase **salt.**) Everybody, write the word (pause) **salt.** ✔
e. (Repeat steps *b–d* for **call** and **fall.**)

EXERCISE 3

Say the sounds, write **come, bark**

a. You're going to write the word (pause) **come.** Say the sounds in **come.** Get ready. (Tap for each sound as the children say:) *k* (pause) *ooo* (pause) *mmm* (pause) *ēēē.*
- (Repeat until firm.)
b. Everybody, write the word (pause) **come.** ✔
c. (Repeat steps *a* and *b* for **bark.**)

EXERCISE 4

Write **sand, hand, bet, said, has, bug**

a. You're going to write the word (pause) **sand.** Think about the sounds in **sand** and write the word. ✔
b. (Repeat step *a* for **hand, bet, said, has,** and **bug.**)

SENTENCE WRITING
EXERCISE 5

Write two sentences

a. Listen to this sentence. **His pig went with him.** Say that sentence. Get ready. (Signal.) *His pig went with him.*
b. Now you're going to say that sentence the slow way. Get ready. (Signal for each word as the children say:) *His* (pause) *pig* (pause) *went* (pause) *with* (pause) *him.*
c. Everybody, write the sentence. Spell each word the right way. ✔
d. (Repeat steps *a–c* for **His cap is in the mud.**)

LESSON 53

SOUND WRITING
EXERCISE 1

Write **al**

a. Everybody, you're going to write the two letters that go together and make the sound **all**. What sound? (Signal.) *All.*
b. Write **al.** ✔

WORD WRITING
EXERCISE 2

Write sound combination words **also, call, ball**

a. (Write on the board: **also, call, ball.**)
b. (Point to **also.**) Everybody, read this word the fast way. Get ready. (Signal.) *Also.* Yes, **also.**
c. Everybody, say the sounds you write for the word (pause) **also.** Get ready. (Touch **al, s, o** as the children say:) *al* (pause) *sss* (pause) *ōōō.*
 • (Repeat until firm.)
d. (Erase **also.**) Everybody, write the word (pause) **also.** ✔
e. (Repeat steps *b–d* for **call** and **ball.**)

EXERCISE 3

Say the sounds, write **how, wish, it, hit, shop, met, hand**

a. You're going to write the word (pause) **how.** Say the sounds in **how.** Get ready. (Tap for each sound as the children say:) *h* (pause) *ooo* (pause) *www.*
 • (Repeat until firm.)
b. Everybody, write the word (pause) **how.** ✔
c. (Repeat steps *a* and *b* for **wish, it, hit, shop, met,** and **hand.**)

EXERCISE 4

Write **do, if**

a. You're going to write the word (pause) **do.** Think about the sounds in **do** and write the word. ✔

b. (Repeat step *a* for **if.**)

SENTENCE WRITING
EXERCISE 5

Write two sentences

a. Listen to this sentence. **She will sell a bell.** Say that sentence. Get ready. (Signal.) *She will sell a bell.*
b. Now you're going to say that sentence the slow way. Get ready. (Signal for each word as the children say:) *She* (pause) *will* (pause) *sell* (pause) *a* (pause) *bell.*
c. Everybody, write the sentence. Spell each word the right way. ✔
d. (Repeat steps *a–c* for **The nut was not fat.**)

LESSON 54

SOUND WRITING
EXERCISE 1

Write **al**

a. Everybody, you're going to write the two letters that go together and make the sound **all**. What sound? (Signal.) *All.*
b. Write **al.** ✔

WORD WRITING
EXERCISE 2

Write sound combination words **tall, salt, wall**

a. (Write on the board: **tall, salt, wall.**)
b. (Point to **tall.**) Everybody, read this word the fast way. Get ready. (Signal.) *Tall.* Yes, **tall.**
c. Everybody, say the sounds you write for the word (pause) **tall.** Get ready. (Touch **t, al, l** as the children say:) *t* (pause) *al* (pause) *lll.*
 • (Repeat until firm.)
d. (Erase **tall.**) Everybody, write the word (pause) **tall.** ✔
e. (Repeat steps *b–d* for **salt** and **wall.**)

EXERCISE 3

Say the sounds, write **fell, card, rug**

a. You're going to write the word (pause) **fell.** Say the sounds in **fell.** Get ready. (Tap for each sound as the children say:) *fff* (pause) *eee* (pause) *lll* (pause) *lll.*

• (Repeat until firm.)

b. Everybody, write the word (pause) **fell. ✔**

c. (Repeat steps *a* and *b* for **card** and **rug.**)

EXERCISE 4

Write **did, big, cap, his, now**

a. You're going to write the word (pause) **did.** Think about the sounds in **did** and write the word. ✔

b. (Repeat step *a* for **big, cap, his,** and **now.**)

SENTENCE WRITING
EXERCISE 5

Write two sentences

a. Listen to this sentence. **The dog will sing with us.** Say that sentence. Get ready. (Signal.) *The dog will sing with us.*

b. Now you're going to say that sentence the slow way. Get ready. (Signal for each word as the children say:) *The* (pause) *dog* (pause) *will* (pause) *sing* (pause) *with* (pause) *us.*

c. Everybody, write the sentence. Spell each word the right way. ✔

d. (Repeat steps *a–c* for **She is on the bus.**)

LESSON 55

WORD WRITING
EXERCISE 1

Say the sounds, write **tall, wall, wish, said, tap**

a. You're going to write the word (pause) **tall.** Say the sounds in **tall.** Get ready. (Tap for each sound as the children say:) *t* (pause) *al* (pause) *lll.*

• (Repeat until firm.)

b. Everybody, write the word (pause) **tall. ✔**

c. (Repeat steps *a* and *b* for **wall, wish, said,** and **tap.**)

EXERCISE 2

Write **them, tell, card, to, ship, cap**

a. You're going to write the word (pause) **them.** Think about the sounds in **them** and write the word. ✔

b. (Repeat step *a* for **tell, card, to, ship,** and **cap.**)

SENTENCE WRITING
EXERCISE 3

Write two sentences

a. Listen to this sentence. **We will hop and sing.** Say that sentence. Get ready. (Signal.) *We will hop and sing.*

b. Now you're going to say that sentence the slow way. Get ready. (Signal for each word as the children say:) *We* (pause) *will* (pause) *hop* (pause) *and* (pause) *sing.*

c. Everybody, write the sentence. Spell each word the right way. ✔

d. (Repeat steps *a–c* for **She did not hit me.**)

LESSON 56

SOUND WRITING
EXERCISE 1

Write **sh, ar, th, al, ing**

a. Everybody, you're going to write the letters that go together and make the sound **sh.** What sound? (Signal.) *sh.*

b. Write **sh. ✔**

c. (Repeat steps *a* and *b* for **ar, th, al,** and **ing.**)

WORD WRITING
EXERCISE 2

Say the sounds, write **salt, card, now, swim, this**

a. You're going to write the word (pause) **salt.** Say the sounds in **salt.** Get ready. (Tap for each sound as the children say:) *sss* (pause) *al* (pause) *t.*

• (Repeat until firm.)

b. Everybody, write the word (pause) **salt.** ✔

c. (Repeat steps *a* and *b* for **card, now, swim,** and **this.**)

EXERCISE 3

Write **call, fun, get, ring, ham**

a. You're going to write the word (pause) **call.** Think about the sounds in **call** and write the word. ✔

b. (Repeat step *a* for **fun, get, ring,** and **ham.**)

SENTENCE WRITING
EXERCISE 4

Write two sentences

a. Listen to this sentence. **That bell did not ring.** Say that sentence. Get ready. (Signal.) *That bell did not ring.*

b. Now you're going to say that sentence the slow way. Get ready. (Signal for each word as the children say:) *That* (pause) *bell* (pause) *did* (pause) *not* (pause) *ring.*

c. Everybody, write the sentence. Spell each word the right way. ✔

d. (Repeat steps *a–c* for **He can run with us.**)

LESSON 57

SOUND WRITING
EXERCISE 1

Write **sh, th, ar, al, ing**

a. Everybody, you're going to write the letters that go together and make the sound **sh.** What sound? (Signal.) *sh.*

b. Write **sh.** ✔

c. (Repeat steps *a* and *b* for **th, ar, al,** and **ing.**)

WORD WRITING
EXERCISE 2

Listen, say the sounds, write **of, stop**

a. You're going to write the word (pause) **of.** When you write the word **of,** you write these sounds: **ooo** (pause) **fff.**

b. Say the sounds you write for (pause) **of.** Get ready. (Tap for each sound as the children say:) *ooo* (pause) *fff.*

• (Repeat until firm.)

c. Everybody, write the word (pause) **of.** ✔

d. (Repeat steps *a–c* for **stop.**)

EXERCISE 3

Say the sounds, write **to, also, went**

a. You're going to write the word (pause) **to.** Say the sounds in **to.** Get ready. (Tap for each sound as the children say:) *t* (pause) *ooo.*

• (Repeat until firm.)

b. Everybody, write the word (pause) **to.** ✔

c. (Repeat steps *a* and *b* for **also** and **went.**)

EXERCISE 4

Write **fish, him, wall, hand, thing**

a. You're going to write the word (pause) **fish.** Think about the sounds in **fish** and write the word. ✔

b. (Repeat step *a* for **him, wall, hand,** and **thing.**)

SENTENCE WRITING
EXERCISE 5

Write two sentences

a. Listen to this sentence. **His card is red.** Say that sentence. Get ready. (Signal.) *His card is red.*

b. Now you're going to say that sentence the slow way. Get ready. (Signal for each word as the children say:) *His* (pause) *card* (pause) *is* (pause) *red.*

c. Everybody, write the sentence. Spell each word the right way. ✔

d. (Repeat steps *a–c* for **This cat has a bell.**)

LESSON 58

SOUND WRITING
EXERCISE 1

Write **th, sh, ar, ing, al**

a. Everybody, you're going to write the letters that go together and make the sound **th.** What sound? (Signal.) *th.*

b. Write **th.** ✔

c. (Repeat steps *a* and *b* for **sh, ar, ing,** and **al.**)

WORD WRITING
EXERCISE 2

Say the sounds, write **said, cup, of, stop**

a. You're going to write the word (pause) **said.** Say the sounds in **said.** Get ready. (Tap for each sound as the children say:) *sss* (pause) *aaa* (pause) *iii* (pause) *d.*

• (Repeat until firm.)

b. Everybody, write the word (pause) **said.** ✔

c. (Repeat steps *a* and *b* for **cup, of,** and **stop.**)

EXERCISE 3

Write **shop, if, big, fall, wet, met, us**

a. You're going to write the word (pause) **shop.** Think about the sounds in **shop** and write the word. ✔

b. (Repeat step *a* for **if, big, fall, wet, met,** and **us.**)

SENTENCE WRITING
EXERCISE 4

Write two sentences

a. Listen to this sentence. **We will sit and sing.** Say that sentence. Get ready. (Signal.) *We will sit and sing.*

b. Now you're going to say that sentence that slow way. Get ready. (Signal for each word as the children say:) *We* (pause) *will* (pause) *sit* (pause) *and* (pause) *sing.*

c. Everybody, write the sentence. Spell each word the right way. ✔

d. (Repeat steps *a–c* for **That cow did not bark.**)

LESSON 59

SOUND WRITING
EXERCISE 1

Introduce sound combination **wh**

a. (Write on the board: **wh.**)

b. (Point to **wh.**) Listen: **wh.** Everybody, tell me the sound these letters make. Get ready. (Signal.) *wh.* Yes, **wh.**

c. (Erase **wh.**) Everybody, write the letters that go together and make the sound **wh.** ✔

WORD WRITING
EXERCISE 2

Say the sounds, write **sing, sand, arm, salt, swim**

a. You're going to write the word (pause) **sing.** Say the sounds in **sing.** Get ready. (Tap for each sound as the children say:) *sss* (pause) *ing.*

• (Repeat until firm.)

b. Everybody, write the word (pause) **sing.** ✔

c. (Repeat steps *a* and *b* for **sand, arm, salt,** and **swim.**)

EXERCISE 3

Write **cap, bed, fish, of, stop**

a. You're going to write the word (pause) **cap.** Think about the sounds in **cap** and write the word. ✔

b. (Repeat step *a* for **bed, fish, of,** and **stop.**)

SENTENCE WRITING
EXERCISE 4

Write two sentences

a. Listen to this sentence. **He will run and fall.** Say that sentence. Get ready. (Signal.) *He will run and fall.*

b. Now you're going to say that sentence the slow way. Get ready. (Signal for each word as the children say:) *He* (pause) *will* (pause) *run* (pause) *and* (pause) *fall.*

c. Everybody, write the sentence. Spell each word the right way. ✔

d. (Repeat steps *a–c* for **A ball fell in the mud.**)

LESSON 60

SOUND WRITING
EXERCISE 1

Introduce sound combination **wh**

a. (Write on the board: **wh.**)

b. (Point to **wh.**) Listen: **wh.** Everybody, tell me the sound these letters make. Get ready. (Signal.) *wh.* Yes, **wh.**

c. (Erase **wh.**) Everybody, write the letters that go together and make the sound **wh.** ✔

WORD WRITING
EXERCISE 2

Write sound combination words **where, when, what**

a. (Write on the board: **where, when, what.**)

b. (Point to **where.**) Everybody, read this word the fast way. Get ready. (Signal.) *Where.* Yes, **where.**

c. Everybody, say the sounds you write for the word (pause) **where.** Get ready. (Touch **wh, e, r, e** as the children say:) *wh* (pause) *eee* (pause) *rrr* (pause) *ēēē.*

• (Repeat until firm.)

d. (Erase **where.**) Everybody, write the word (pause) **where.** ✔

e. (Repeat steps *b–d* for **when** and **what.**)

EXERCISE 3

Say the sounds, write **him, with, pill**

a. You're going to write the word (pause) **him.** Say the sounds in **him.** Get ready. (Tap for each sound as the children say:) *h* (pause) *iii* (pause) *mmm.*

• (Repeat until firm.)

b. Everybody, write the word (pause) **him.** ✔

c. (Repeat steps *a* and *b* for **with** and **pill.**)

EXERCISE 4

Write **fed, red, car, stop, also**

a. You're going to write the word (pause) **fed.** Think about the sounds in **fed** and write the word. ✔

b. (Repeat step *a* for **red, car, stop,** and **also.**)

SENTENCE WRITING
EXERCISE 5

Write two sentences

a. Listen to this sentence. **His cap fell in the sand.** Say that sentence. Get ready. (Signal.) *His cap fell in the sand.*

b. Now you're going to say that sentence the slow way. Get ready. (Signal for each word as the children say:) *His* (pause) *cap* (pause) *fell* (pause) *in* (pause) *the* (pause) *sand.*

c. Everybody, write the sentence. Spell each word the right way. ✔

d. (Repeat steps *a–c* for **This pig can run.**)

LESSON 61

SOUND WRITING
EXERCISE 1

Introduce sound combination **wh**

a. (Write on the board: **wh.**)

b. (Point to **wh.**) Everybody, tell me the sound these letters make. Get ready. (Signal.) *wh.* Yes, **wh.**

c. (Erase **wh.**) Everybody, write the letters that go together and make the sound **wh.** ✔

WORD WRITING
EXERCISE 2

Write sound combination words **when, where, what**

a. (Write on the board: **when, where, what.**)

b. (Point to **when.**) Everybody, read this word the fast way. Get ready. (Signal.) *When.* Yes, **when.**

c. Everybody, say the sounds you write for the word (pause) **when.** Get ready. (Touch **wh, e, n** as the children say:) *wh* (pause) *eee* (pause) *nnn.*

- (Repeat until firm.)

d. (Erase **when.**) Everybody, write the word (pause) **when.** ✔

e. (Repeat steps *b–d* for **where** and **what.**)

EXERCISE 3

Say the sounds, write **thing, now, dish**

a. You're going to write the word (pause) **thing.** Say the sounds in **thing.** Get ready. (Tap for each sound as the children say:) *th* (pause) *ing.*

- (Repeat until firm.)

b. Everybody, write the word (pause) **thing.** ✔

c. (Repeat steps *a* and *b* for **now** and **dish.**)

EXERCISE 4

Write **ten, sand, of, hen, bug, salt**

a. You're going to write the word (pause) **ten.** Think about the sounds in **ten** and write the word. ✔

b. (Repeat step *a* for **sand, of, hen, bug,** and **salt.**)

SENTENCE WRITING
EXERCISE 5

Write two sentences

a. Listen to this sentence. **The mop is on the rug.** Say that sentence. Get ready. (Signal.) *The mop is on the rug.*

b. Now you're going to say that sentence the slow way. Get ready. (Signal for each word as the children say:) *The* (pause) *mop* (pause) *is* (pause) *on* (pause) *the* (pause) *rug.*

c. Everybody, write the sentence. Spell each word the right way. ✔

d. (Repeat steps *a–c* for **His dog has a bell.**)

LESSON 62

SOUND WRITING
EXERCISE 1

Write **wh**

a. Everybody, you're going to write the letters that go together and make the sound **wh.** What sound? (Signal.) *wh.*

b. Write **wh.** ✔

WORD WRITING
EXERCISE 2

Write sound combination words **when, what, where**

a. (Write on the board: **when, what, where.**)

b. (Point to **when.**) Everybody, read this word the fast way. Get ready. (Signal.) *When.* Yes, **when.**

c. Everybody, say the sounds you write for the word (pause) **when.** Get ready. (Touch **wh, e, n** as the children say:) *wh* (pause) *eee* (pause) *nnn.*

- (Repeat until firm.)

d. (Erase **when.**) Everybody, write the word (pause) **when.** ✔

e. (Repeat steps *b–d* for **what** and **where.**)

EXERCISE 3

Say the sounds, write **wish, hut, come, said**

a. You're going to write the word (pause) **wish.** Say the sounds in **wish.** Get ready. (Tap for each sound as the children say:) *www* (pause) *iii* (pause) *sh.*

41

- (Repeat until firm.)
b. Everybody, write the word (pause) **wish.** ✔
c. (Repeat steps *a* and *b* for **hut, come,** and **said.**)

EXERCISE 4

Write **bark, to, but, hill**

a. You're going to write the word (pause) **bark.** Think about the sounds in **bark** and write the word. ✔
b. (Repeat step *a* for **to, but,** and **hill.**)

SENTENCE WRITING
EXERCISE 5

Write two sentences

a. Listen to this sentence. **His pig can sing.** Say that sentence. Get ready. (Signal.) *His pig can sing.*
b. Now you're going to say that sentence the slow way. Get ready. (Signal for each word as the children say:) *His* (pause) *pig* (pause) *can* (pause) *sing.*
c. Everybody, write the sentence. Spell each word the right way. ✔
d. (Repeat steps *a*–*c* for **That hen is not tall.**)

LESSON 63

SOUND WRITING
EXERCISE 1

Write **wh**

a. Everybody, you're going to write the letters that go together and make the sound **wh.** What sound? (Signal.) *wh.*
b. Write **wh.** ✔

WORD WRITING
EXERCISE 2

Write sound combination words **what, where, when**

a. (Write on the board: **what, where, when.**)
b. (Point to **what.**) Everybody, read this word the fast way. Get ready. (Signal.) *What.* Yes, **what.**

c. Everybody, say the sounds you write for the word (pause) **what.** Get ready. (Touch **wh, a, t** as the children say:) *wh* (pause) *aaa* (pause) *t.*
- (Repeat until firm.)
d. (Erase **what.**) Everybody, write the word (pause) **what.** ✔
e. (Repeat steps *b*–*d* for **where** and **when.**)

EXERCISE 3

Listen, say the sounds, write **are**

a. You're going to write the word (pause) **are.** When you write the word **are,** you write these sounds: **ar** (pause) **ēēē.**
b. Say the sounds you write for (pause) **are.** Get ready. (Tap for each sound as the children say:) *ar* (pause) *ēēē.*
- (Repeat until firm.)
c. Everybody, write the word (pause) **are.** ✔

EXERCISE 4

Say the sounds, write **stop, if, ball**

a. You're going to write the word (pause) **stop.** Say the sounds in **stop.** Get ready. (Tap for each sound as the children say:) *sss* (pause) *t* (pause) *ooo* (pause) *p.*
- (Repeat until firm.)
b. Everybody, write the word (pause) **stop.** ✔
c. (Repeat steps *a* and *b* for **if** and **ball.**)

EXERCISE 5

Write **tall, cow, us, bus**

a. You're going to write the word (pause) **tall.** Think about the sounds in **tall** and write the word. ✔
b. (Repeat step *a* for **cow, us,** and **bus.**)

SENTENCE WRITING
EXERCISE 6

Write two sentences

a. Listen to this sentence. **She will sit with me.** Say that sentence. Get ready. (Signal.) *She will sit with me.*
b. Now you're going to say that sentence the slow way. Get ready. (Signal for each word as the children say:) *She* (pause) *will* (pause) *sit* (pause) *with* (pause) *me.*

c. Everybody, write the sentence. Spell each word the right way. ✔

d. (Repeat steps *a–c* for **That hen is in the sun.**)

LESSON 64

WORD WRITING
EXERCISE 1

Listen, say the sounds, write **are**

a. You're going to write the word (pause) **are.** When you write the word **are,** you write these sounds: **ar** (pause) ēēē.

b. Say the sounds you write for (pause) **are.** Get ready. (Tap for each sound as the children say:) *ar* (pause) *ēēē.*

• (Repeat until firm.)

c. Everybody, write the word (pause) **are.** ✔

EXERCISE 2

Say the sounds, write **barn, stop, went, what, where**

a. You're going to write the word (pause) **barn.** Say the sounds in **barn.** Get ready. (Tap for each sound as the children say:)
b (pause) *ar* (pause) *nnn.*

• (Repeat until firm.)

b. Everybody, write the word (pause) **barn.** ✔

c. (Repeat steps *a* and *b* for **stop, went, what,** and **where.**)

EXERCISE 3

Write **far, hill, ship, cop, ring**

a. You're going to write the word (pause) **far.** Think about the sounds in **far** and write the word. ✔

b. (Repeat step *a* for **hill, ship, cop,** and **ring.**)

SENTENCE WRITING
EXERCISE 4

Write two sentences

a. Listen to this sentence. **This ball is big.** Say that sentence. Get ready. (Signal.) *This ball is big.*

b. Now you're going to say that sentence the slow way. Get ready. (Signal for each word as the children say:) *This* (pause) *ball* (pause) *is* (pause) *big.*

c. Everybody, write the sentence. Spell each word the right way. ✔

d. (Repeat steps *a–c* for **She did not call him.**)

LESSON 65

WORD WRITING
EXERCISE 1

Say the sounds, write **are, when, also, where, come**

a. You're going to write the word (pause) **are.** Say the sounds in **are.** Get ready. (Tap for each sound as the children say:) *ar* (pause) *ēēē.*

• (Repeat until firm.)

b. Everybody, write the word (pause) **are.** ✔

c. (Repeat steps *a* and *b* for **when, also, where,** and **come.**)

EXERCISE 2

Write **up, cup, sand, ham, met, wall**

a. You're going to write the word (pause) **up.** Think about the sounds in **up** and write the word. ✔

b. (Repeat step *a* for **cup, sand, ham, met,** and **wall.**)

SENTENCE WRITING
EXERCISE 3

Write two sentences

a. Listen to this sentence. **His bell did not ring.** Say that sentence. Get ready. (Signal.) *His bell did not ring.*

b. Now you're going to say that sentence the slow way. Get ready. (Signal for each word as the children say:) *His* (pause) *bell* (pause) *did* (pause) *not* (pause) *ring.*

c. Everybody, write the sentence. Spell each word the right way. ✔

d. (Repeat steps *a–c* for **This cow has a barn.**)

SOUND WRITING
EXERCISE 1

Introduce sound combination **er**

a. (Write on the board: **er.**)

b. (Point to **er.**) Everybody, tell me the sound these letters make. Get ready. (Signal.) *er.* Yes, **er.**

c. (Erase **er.**) Everybody, write the letters that go together and make the sound **er.** ✔

WORD WRITING
EXERCISE 2

Say the sounds, write **stop, dug, salt, swim**

a. You're going to write the word (pause) **stop.** Say the sounds in **stop.** Get ready. (Tap for each sound as the children say:) *sss* (pause) *t* (pause) *ooo* (pause) *p.*
* (Repeat until firm.)

b. Everybody, write the word (pause) **stop.** ✔

c. (Repeat steps *a* and *b* for **dug, salt,** and **swim.**)

EXERCISE 3

Write **are, cop, shop, what, then, park**

a. You're going to write the word (pause) **are.** Think about the sounds in **are** and write the word. ✔

b. (Repeat step *a* for **cop, shop, what, then,** and **park.**)

SENTENCE WRITING
EXERCISE 4

Write two sentences

a. Listen to this sentence. **His dog has the ham.** Say that sentence. Get ready. (Signal.) *His dog has the ham.*

b. Now you're going to say that sentence the slow way. Get ready. (Signal for each word as the children say:) *His* (pause) *dog* (pause) *has* (pause) *the* (pause) *ham.*

c. Everybody, write the sentence. Spell each word the right way. ✔

d. (Repeat steps *a–c* for **The pig ran up the hill.**)

SOUND WRITING
EXERCISE 1

Introduce sound combination **er**

a. (Write on the board: **er.**)

b. (Point to **er.**) Everybody, tell me the sound these letters make. Get ready. (Signal.) *er.* Yes, **er.**

c. (Erase **er.**) Everybody, write the letters that go together and make the sound **er.** ✔

WORD WRITING
EXERCISE 2

Write sound combination words **ever, never, other, her**

a. (Write on the board: **ever, never, other, her.**)

b. (Point to **ever.**) Everybody, read this word the fast way. Get ready. (Signal.) *Ever.* Yes, **ever.**

c. Everybody, say the sounds you write for the word (pause) **ever.** Get ready. (Touch **e, v, er** as the children say:) *eee* (pause) *vvv* (pause) *er.*
* (Repeat until firm.)

d. (Erase **ever.**) Everybody, write the word (pause) **ever.** ✔

e. (Repeat steps *b–d* for **never, other,** and **her.**)

EXERCISE 3

Say the sounds, write **how, do, with**

a. You're going to write the word (pause) **how.** Say the sounds in **how.** Get ready. (Tap for each sound as the children say:) *h* (pause) *ooo* (pause) *www.*
- (Repeat until firm.)
b. Everybody, write the word (pause) **how. ✔**
c. (Repeat steps *a* and *b* for **do** and **with.**)

EXERCISE 4

Write **when, of, tell, fell, big**

a. You're going to write the word (pause) **when.** Think about the sounds in **when** and write the word. **✔**
b. (Repeat step *a* for **of, tell, fell,** and **big.**)

SENTENCE WRITING
EXERCISE 5

Write two sentences

a. Listen to this sentence. **The man has the cup.** Say that sentence. Get ready. (Signal.) *The man has the cup.*
b. Now you're going to say that sentence the slow way. Get ready. (Signal for each word as the children say:) *The* (pause) *man* (pause) *has* (pause) *the* (pause) *cup.*
c. Everybody, write the sentence. Spell each word the right way. **✔**
d. (Repeat steps *a–c* for **A cow ran up the hill.**)

LESSON 68

SOUND WRITING
EXERCISE 1

Introduce sound combination **er**

a. (Write on the board: **er.**)
b. (Point to **er.**) Everybody, tell me the sound these letters make. Get ready. (Signal.) *er.* Yes, **er.**

c. (Erase **er.**) Everybody, write the letters that go together and make the sound **er. ✔**

WORD WRITING
EXERCISE 2

Write sound combination words **her, other, never**

a. (Write on the board: **her, other, never.**)
b. (Point to **her.**) Everybody, read this word the fast way. Get ready. (Signal.) *Her.* Yes, **her.**
c. Everybody, say the sounds you write for the word (pause) **her.** Get ready. (Touch **h, er** as the children say:) *h* (pause) *er.*
- (Repeat until firm.)
d. (Erase **her.**) Everybody, write the word (pause) **her. ✔**
e. (Point to **other.**) Everybody, read this word the fast way. Get ready. (Signal.) *Other.* Yes, **other.**
f. Everybody, say the sounds you write for the word (pause) **other.** Get ready. (Touch **o, th, er** as the children say:) *ooo* (pause) *th* (pause) *er.*
- (Repeat until firm.)
g. (Erase **other.**) Everybody, write the word (pause) **other. ✔**
h. (Repeat steps *e–g* for **never.**)

EXERCISE 3

Say the sounds, write **what, sell, had**

a. You're going to write the word (pause) **what.** Say the sounds in **what.** Get ready. (Tap for each sound as the children say:) *wh* (pause) *aaa* (pause) *t.*
- (Repeat until firm.)
b. Everybody, write the word (pause) **what. ✔**
c. (Repeat steps *a* and *b* for **sell** and **had.**)

EXERCISE 4

Write **it, hit, fit, top, men, at**

a. You're going to write the word (pause) **it.** Think about the sounds in **it** and write the word. **✔**
b. (Repeat step *a* for **hit, fit, top, men,** and **at.**)

45

SENTENCE WRITING
EXERCISE 5

Write two sentences

a. Listen to this sentence. **That fish will get fat.** Say that sentence. Get ready. (Signal.) *That fish will get fat.*

b. Now you're going to say that sentence the slow way. Get ready. (Signal for each word as the children say:) *That* (pause) *fish* (pause) *will* (pause) *get* (pause) *fat.*

c. Everybody, write the sentence. Spell each word the right way. ✔

d. (Repeat steps *a–c* for **His dog can run and bark.**)

LESSON 69

SOUND WRITING
EXERCISE 1

Write **er**

a. Everybody, you're going to write the letters that go together and make the sound **er.** What sound? (Signal.) *er.*

b. Write **er.** ✔

WORD WRITING
EXERCISE 2

Write sound combination words **never, other, ever, her**

a. (Write on the board: **never, other, ever, her.**)

b. (Point to **never.**) Everybody, read this word the fast way. Get ready. (Signal.) *Never.* Yes, **never.**

c. Everybody, say the sounds you write for the word (pause) **never.** Get ready. (Touch **n, e, v, er** as the children say:) *nnn* (pause) *eee* (pause) *vvv* (pause) *er.*

• (Repeat until firm.)

d. (Erase **never.**) Everybody, write the word (pause) **never.** ✔

e. (Repeat steps *b–d* for **other, ever,** and **her.**)

EXERCISE 3

Say the sounds, write **pet, shot, got**

a. You're going to write the word (pause) **pet.** Say the sounds in **pet.** Get ready. (Tap for each sound as the children say:) *p* (pause) *eee* (pause) *t.*

• (Repeat until firm.)

b. Everybody, write the word (pause) **pet.** ✔

c. (Repeat steps *a* and *b* for **shot** and **got.**)

EXERCISE 4

Write **pit, had, when, farm**

a. You're going to write the word (pause) **pit.** Think about the sounds in **pit** and write the word. ✔

b. (Repeat step *a* for **had, when,** and **farm.**)

SENTENCE WRITING
EXERCISE 5

Write two sentences

a. Listen to this sentence. **We did not get wet.** Say that sentence. Get ready. (Signal.) *We did not get wet.*

b. Now you're going to say that sentence the slow way. Get ready. (Signal for each word as the children say:) *We* (pause) *did* (pause) *not* (pause) *get* (pause) *wet.*

c. Everybody, write the sentence. Spell each word the right way. ✔

d. (Repeat steps *a–c* for **She has a dog and a cat.**)

LESSON 70

SOUND WRITING
EXERCISE 1

Write **er**

a. Everybody, you're going to write the letters that go together and make the sound **er.** What sound? (Signal.) *er.*

b. Write **er.** ✔

WORD WRITING
EXERCISE 2

Write sound combination words **ever, other, her, never**

a. (Write on the board: **ever, other, her, never.**)
b. (Point to **ever.**) Everybody, read this word the fast way. Get ready. (Signal.) *Ever.* Yes, **ever.**
c. Everybody, say the sounds you write for the word (pause) **ever.** Get ready. (Touch **e, v, er** as the children say:) *eee* (pause) *vvv* (pause) *er.*
• (Repeat until firm.)
d. (Erase **ever.**) Everybody, write the word (pause) **ever.** ✔
e. (Repeat steps *b–d* for **other, her,** and **never.**)

EXERCISE 3

Say the sounds, write **thing, got, wish, where**

a. You're going to write the word (pause) **thing.** Say the sounds in **thing.** Get ready. (Tap for each sound as the children say:) *th* (pause) *ing.*
• (Repeat until firm.)
b. Everybody, write the word (pause) **thing.** ✔
c. (Repeat steps *a* and *b* for **got, wish,** and **where.**)

EXERCISE 4

Write **shot, salt, went, get, is**

a. You're going to write the word (pause) **shot.** Think about the sounds in **shot** and write the word. ✔
b. (Repeat step *a* for **salt, went, get,** and **is.**)

SENTENCE WRITING
EXERCISE 5

Write two sentences

a. Listen to this sentence. **He has a nut and a cat.** Say that sentence. Get ready. (Signal.) *He has a nut and a cat.*

b. Now you're going to say that sentence the slow way. Get ready. (Signal for each word as the children say:) *He* (pause) *has* (pause) *a* (pause) *nut* (pause) *and* (pause) *a* (pause) *cat.*
c. Everybody, write the sentence. Spell each word the right way. ✔
d. (Repeat steps *a–c* for **We are on a farm.**)

LESSON 71

SOUND WRITING
EXERCISE 1

Write **wh, er, al**

a. Everybody, you're going to write the two letters that go together and make the sound **wh.** What sound? (Signal.) *wh.*
b. Write **wh.** ✔
c. (Repeat steps *a* and *b* for **er** and **al.**)

WORD WRITING
EXERCISE 2

Say the sounds, write **other, card, leg, beg**

a. You're going to write the word (pause) **other.** Say the sounds in **other.** Get ready. (Tap for each sound as the children say:) *ooo* (pause) *th* (pause) *er.*
• (Repeat until firm.)
b. Everybody, write the word (pause) **other.** ✔
c. (Repeat steps *a* and *b* for **card, leg,** and **beg.**)

EXERCISE 3

Write **her, what, up, where, come, with, also**

a. You're going to write the word (pause) **her.** Think about the sounds in **her** and write the word. ✔
b. (Repeat step *a* for **what, up, where, come, with,** and **also.**)

SENTENCE WRITING
EXERCISE 4

Write two sentences

a. Listen to this sentence. **She has a hat and a rat.** Say that sentence. Get ready. (Signal.) *She has a hat and a rat.*

b. Now you're going to say that sentence the slow way. Get ready. (Signal for each word as the children say:) *She* (pause) *has* (pause) *a* (pause) *hat* (pause) *and* (pause) *a* (pause) *rat.*

c. Everybody, write the sentence. Spell each word the right way. ✔

d. (Repeat steps *a–c* for **We are on the ship.**)

LESSON 72

SOUND WRITING
EXERCISE 1

Write **wh, al, er**

a. Everybody, you're going to write the two letters that go together and make the sound **wh.** What sound? (Signal.) *wh.*

b. Write **wh.** ✔

c. (Repeat steps *a* and *b* for **al** and **er.**)

WORD WRITING
EXERCISE 2

Say the sounds, write **ring, leg, said, other, brother**

a. You're going to write the word (pause) **ring.** Say the sounds in **ring.** Get ready. (Tap for each sound as the children say:) *rrr* (pause) *ing.*

• (Repeat until firm.)

b. Everybody, write the word (pause) **ring.** ✔

c. (Repeat steps *a* and *b* for **leg, said, other,** and **brother.**)

EXERCISE 3

Write **when, what, shot, met, got, them**

a. You're going to write the word (pause) **when.** Think about the sounds in **when** and write the word. ✔

b. (Repeat step *a* for **what, shot, met, got,** and **them.**)

SENTENCE WRITING
EXERCISE 4

Write three sentences

a. Listen to this sentence. **That bus will not stop.** Say that sentence. Get ready. (Signal.) *That bus will not stop.*

b. Now you're going to say that sentence the slow way. Get ready. (Signal for each word as the children say:) *That* (pause) *bus* (pause) *will* (pause) *not* (pause) *stop.*

c. Everybody, write the sentence. Spell each word the right way. ✔

d. (Repeat steps *a–c* for **The men are sad** and **She has a dog.**)

LESSON 73

SOUND WRITING
EXERCISE 1

Write **al, wh, er**

a. Everybody, you're going to write the two letters that go together and make the sound **all.** What sound? (Signal.) *All.*

b. Write **al.** ✔

c. (Repeat steps *a* and *b* for **wh** and **er.**)

WORD WRITING
EXERCISE 2

Say the sounds, write **rug, bug, brother, ever**

a. You're going to write the word (pause) **rug.** Say the sounds in **rug.** Get ready. (Tap for each sound as the children say:) *rrr* (pause) *uuu* (pause) *g.*

- (Repeat until firm.)
b. Everybody, write the word (pause) **rug.** ✔
c. (Repeat steps *a* and *b* for **bug, brother, and ever.**)

EXERCISE 3

Write **where, shot, beg, top, cop, other**

a. You're going to write the word (pause) **where.** Think about the sounds in **where** and write the word. ✔
b. (Repeat step *a* for **shot, beg, top, cop, and other.**)

SENTENCE WRITING
EXERCISE 4

Write three sentences

a. Listen to this sentence. **His car will not run.** Say that sentence. Get ready. (Signal.) *His car will not run.*
b. Now you're going to say that sentence the slow way. Get ready. (Signal for each word as the children say:) *His* (pause) *car* (pause) *will* (pause) *not* (pause) *run.*
c. Everybody, write the sentence. Spell each word the right way. ✔
d. (Repeat steps *a–c* for **She did not fall** and **Her dog is fat.**)

LESSON 74

WORD WRITING
EXERCISE 1

Say the sounds, write **never, after, also, other, mother**

a. You're going to write the word (pause) **never.** Say the sounds in **never.** Get ready. (Tap for each sound as the children say:) *nnn* (pause) *eee* (pause) *vvv* (pause) *er.*
- (Repeat until firm.)
b. Everybody, write the word (pause) **never.** ✔

c. (Repeat steps *a* and *b* for **after, also, other,** and **mother.**)

EXERCISE 2

Write **to, what, arm, when, brother, had**

a. You're going to write the word (pause) **to.** Think about the sounds in **to** and write the word. ✔
b. (Repeat step *a* for **what, arm, when, brother, had.**)

SENTENCE WRITING
EXERCISE 3

Write three sentences

a. Listen to this sentence. **That cop can sing.** Say that sentence. Get ready. (Signal.) *That cop can sing.*
b. Now you're going to say that sentence the slow way. Get ready. (Signal for each word as the children say:) *That* (pause) *cop* (pause) *can* (pause) *sing.*
c. Everybody, write the sentence. Spell each word the right way. ✔
d. (Repeat steps *a–c* for **He did not hit her** and **She has a fish.**)

LESSON 75

WORD WRITING
EXERCISE 1

Say the sounds, write **are, mother**

a. You're going to write the word (pause) **are.** Say the sounds in **are.** Get ready. (Tap for each sound as the children say:) *ar* (pause) *ēēē.*
- (Repeat until firm.)
b. Everybody, write the word (pause) **are.** ✔
c. (Repeat steps *a* and *b* for **mother.**)

EXERCISE 2

Write **him, with, went, fun, got, after, tall, cow**

a. You're going to write the word (pause) **him.** Think about the sounds in **him** and write the word. ✔

b. (Repeat step *a* for **with, went, fun, got, after, tall,** and **cow.**)

SENTENCE WRITING
EXERCISE 3

Write three sentences

a. Listen to this sentence. **We will never run.** Say that sentence. Get ready. (Signal.) *We will never run.*

b. Now you're going to say that sentence the slow way. Get ready. (Signal for each word as the children say:) *We* (pause) *will* (pause) *never* (pause) *run.*

c. Everybody, write the sentence. Spell each word the right way. ✔

d. (Repeat steps *a–c* for **He can hop and sing** and **We are on the ship.**)

LESSON 76

WORD WRITING
EXERCISE 1

Say the sounds, write **her, win, said, where, has**

a. You're going to write the word (pause) **her.** Say the sounds in **her.** Get ready. (Tap for each sound as the children say:) *h* (pause) *er.*

• (Repeat until firm.)

b. Everybody, write the word (pause) **her.** ✔

c. (Repeat steps *a* and *b* for **win, said, where,** and **has.**)

EXERCISE 2

Write **bark, stop, ever, sing, of, dish**

a. You're going to write the word (pause) **bark.** Think about the sounds in **bark** and write the word. ✔

b. (Repeat step *a* for **stop, ever, sing, of,** and **dish.**)

SENTENCE WRITING
EXERCISE 3

Write three sentences

a. Listen to this sentence. **That man went with him.** Say that sentence. Get ready. (Signal.) *That man went with him.*

b. Now you're going to say that sentence the slow way. Get ready. (Signal for each word as the children say:) *That* (pause) *man* (pause) *went* (pause) *with* (pause) *him.*

c. Everybody, write the sentence. Spell each word the right way. ✔

d. (Repeat steps *a–c* for **The men are in the barn** and **He has a ball.**)

LESSON 77

SOUND WRITING
EXERCISE 1

Introduce sound combination **ck**

a. (Write on the board: **ck.**)

b. (Point to **ck.**) Everybody, tell me the sound these letters make. Get ready. (Signal.) *k.* Yes, **k.**

c. (Erase **ck.**) Everybody, write the letters that go together and make the sound **k.** ✔

WORD WRITING
EXERCISE 2

Say the sounds, write **hand, when, ship**

a. You're going to write the word (pause) **hand.** Say the sounds in **hand.** Get ready. (Tap for each sound as the children say:) *h* (pause) *aaa* (pause) *nnn* (pause) *d.*

• (Repeat until firm.)

b. Everybody, write the word (pause) **hand.** ✔

c. (Repeat steps *a* and *b* for **when** and **ship.**)

EXERCISE 3

Write **top, hop, cop, swim, other, brother, card, if**

a. You're going to write the word (pause) **top.** Think about the sounds in **top** and write the word. ✔

b. (Repeat step *a* for **hop, cop, swim, other, brother, card,** and **if.**)

SENTENCE WRITING
EXERCISE 4

Write three sentences

a. Listen to this sentence. **That ham is on the dish.** Say that sentence. Get ready. (Signal.) *That ham is on the dish.* Now you're going to say that sentence the slow way. Get ready. (Signal for each word as the children say:) *That* (pause) *ham* (pause) *is* (pause) *on* (pause) *the* (pause) *dish.*

b. Everybody, write the sentence. Spell each word the right way. ✔

c. (Repeat steps *a–c* for **This dog can dig** and **She went with him.**)

LESSON 78

SOUND WRITING
EXERCISE 1

Introduce sound combination **ck**

a. (Write on the board: **ck.**)

b. (Point to **ck.**) Everybody, tell me the sound these letters make. Get ready. (Signal.) *k.* Yes, **k.**

c. (Erase **ck.**) Everybody, write the letters that go together and make the sound **ck.** ✔

WORD WRITING
EXERCISE 2

Write sound combination words **rock, sock, sack, pick**

a. (Write on the board: **rock, sock, sack,** and **pick.**)

b. (Point to **rock.**) Everybody, read this word the fast way. Get ready. (Signal.) *Rock.* Yes, **rock.**

c. Everybody, say the sounds you write for the word (pause) **rock.** Get ready. (Touch **r, o, ck** as the children say:) *rrr* (pause) *ooo* (pause) *k.*

• (Repeat until firm.)

d. (Erase **rock.**) Everybody, write the word (pause) **rock.** ✔

e. (Repeat steps *b–d* for **sock, sack,** and **pick.**)

EXERCISE 3

Say the sounds, write **how, bark, where**

a. You're going to write the word (pause) **how.** Say the sounds in **how.** Get ready. (Tap for each sound as the children say:) *h* (pause) *ooo* (pause) *www.*

• (Repeat until firm.)

b. Everybody, write the word (pause) **how.** ✔

c. (Repeat steps *a* and *b* for **bark** and **where.**)

EXERCISE 4

Write **brother, mother, wall, call**

a. You're going to write the word (pause) **brother.** Think about the sounds in **brother** and write the word. ✔

b. (Repeat step *a* for **mother, wall,** and **call.**)

SENTENCE WRITING
EXERCISE 5

Write two sentences

a. Listen to this sentence. **A hen can not bark.** Say that sentence. Get ready. (Signal.) *A hen can not bark.*

b. Now you're going to say that sentence the slow way. Get ready. (Signal for each word as the children say:) *A* (pause) *hen* (pause) *can* (pause) *not* (pause) *bark.*

c. Everybody, write the sentence. Spell each word the right way. ✔

d. (Repeat steps *a–c* for **He went with her.**)

LESSON 79

SOUND WRITING
EXERCISE 1

Write **ck**

a. Everybody, you're going to write the two letters that go together and make the sound **k.** What sound? (Signal.) *k.*

b. Write **ck.** ✔

WORD WRITING
EXERCISE 2

Write sound combination words **pack, back, rock, sock**

a. (Write on the board: **pack, back, rock, sock.**)

b. (Point to **pack.**) Everybody, read this word the fast way. Get ready. (Signal.) *Pack.* Yes, **pack.**

c. Everybody, say the sounds you write for the word (pause) **pack.** Get ready. (Touch **p, a, ck** as the children say:) *p* (pause) *aaa* (pause) *k.*

• (Repeat until firm.)

d. (Erase **pack.**) Everybody, write the word (pause) **pack.** ✔

e. (Repeat steps *b–d* for **back, rock,** and **sock.**)

EXERCISE 3

Say the sounds, write **with, cup, went, bag**

a. You're going to write the word (pause) **with.** Say the sounds in **with.** Get ready. (Tap for each sound as the children say:) *www* (pause) *iii* (pause) *th.*

• (Repeat until firm.)

b. Everybody, write the word (pause) **with.** ✔

c. (Repeat steps *a* and *b* for **cup, went,** and **bag.**)

EXERCISE 4

Write **salt, bet, met, after**

a. You're going to write the word (pause) **salt.** Think about the sounds in **salt** and write the word. ✔

b. (Repeat step *a* for **bet, met,** and **after.**)

SENTENCE WRITING
EXERCISE 5

Write two sentences

a. Listen to this sentence. **Her dog has a red ball.** Say that sentence. Get ready. (Signal.) *Her dog has a red ball.*

b. Now you're going to say that sentence the slow way. Get ready. (Signal for each word as the children say:) *Her* (pause) *dog* (pause) *has* (pause) *a* (pause) *red* (pause) *ball.*

c. Everybody, write the sentence. Spell each word the right way. ✔

d. (Repeat steps *a–c* for **The other hat is big.**)

LESSON 80

SOUND WRITING
EXERCISE 1

Write **ck**

a. Everybody, you're going to write the two letters that go together and make the sound **k.** What sound? (Signal.) *k.*

b. Write **ck.** ✔

WORD WRITING
EXERCISE 2

Write sound combination words **stuck, truck, luck, duck**

a. (Write on the board: **stuck, truck, luck, duck.**)

b. (Point to **stuck.**) Everybody, read this word the fast way. Get ready. (Signal.) *Stuck.* Yes, **stuck.**

c. Everybody, say the sounds you write for the word (pause) **stuck.** Get ready. (Touch **s, t, u, ck** as the children say:) *sss* (pause) *t* (pause) *uuu* (pause) *k.*

• (Repeat until firm.)

d. (Erase **stuck.**) Everybody, write the word (pause) **stuck.** ✔

e. (Repeat steps *b–d* for **truck, luck,** and **duck.**)

EXERCISE 3

Say the sounds, write **never, where, said, nut**

a. You're going to write the word (pause) **never.** Say the sounds in **never.** Get ready. (Tap for each sound as the children say:) *nnn* (pause) *eee* (pause) *vvv* (pause) *er.*

• (Repeat until firm.)

b. Everybody, write the word (pause) **never.** ✔

c. (Repeat steps *a* and *b* for **where, said,** and **nut.**)

SENTENCE WRITING
EXERCISE 4

Write two sentences

a. Listen to this sentence. **This ball is red.**
Say that sentence. Get ready. (Signal.) *This ball is red.*

b. Now you're going to say that sentence the slow way. Get ready. (Signal for each word as the children say:)
This (pause) *ball* (pause) *is* (pause) *red.*

c. Everybody, write the sentence. Spell each word the right way. ✔

d. (Repeat steps *a–c* for **The other dog is fat.**)

LESSON 81

SOUND WRITING
EXERCISE 1

Write **er, al, ck**

a. Everybody, you're going to write the two letters that go together and make the sound **er.** What sound? (Signal.) *er.*

b. Write **er.** ✔

c. (Repeat steps *a* and *b* for **al** and **ck.**)

WORD WRITING
EXERCISE 2

Write sound combination words **lick, rock, luck, back**

a. (Write on the board: **lick, rock, luck, back.**)

b. (Point to **lick.**) Everybody, read this word the fast way. Get ready. (Signal.) *Lick.* Yes, **lick.**

c. Everybody, say the sounds you write for the word (pause) **lick.** Get ready. (Touch **l, i, ck** as the children say:) *lll* (pause) *iii* (pause) *k.*

• (Repeat until firm.)

d. (Erase **lick.**) Everybody, write the word (pause) **lick.** ✔

e. (Repeat steps *b–d* for **rock, luck,** and **back.**)

EXERCISE 3

Say the sounds, write **when, also, stop, of**

a. You're going to write the word (pause) **when.** Say the sounds in **when.** Get ready. (Tap for each sound as the children say:) *wh* (pause) *eee* (pause) *nnn.*

• (Repeat until firm.)

b. Everybody, write the word (pause) **when.** ✔

c. (Repeat steps *a* and *b* for **also, stop,** and **of.**)

SENTENCE WRITING
EXERCISE 4

Write two sentences

a. Listen to this sentence. **They also come with us.**
Say that sentence. Get ready. (Signal.) *They also come with us.*

b. Now you're going to say that sentence the slow way. Get ready. (Signal for each word as the children say:) *They* (pause) *also* (pause) *come* (pause) *with* (pause) *us.*

c. Everybody, write the sentence. Spell each word the right way. ✔

d. (Repeat steps *a–c* for **We are on a ship.**)

LESSON 82

SOUND WRITING
EXERCISE 1

Write **ing, ck, sh**

a. Everybody, you're going to write the letters that go together and make the sound **ing.** What sound? (Signal.) *ing.*

b. Write **ing.** ✔

c. (Repeat steps *a* and *b* for **ck** and **sh.**)

WORD WRITING
EXERCISE 2

Write sound combination words **her, other, never**

a. (Write on the board: **her, other, never.**)

b. (Point to **her.**) Everybody, read this word the fast way. Get ready. (Signal.) *Her.* Yes, **her.**

c. Everybody, say the sounds you write for the word (pause) **her.** Get ready. (Touch **h, er** as the children say:) *h* (pause) *er.*

• (Repeat until firm.)

d. (Erase **her.**) Everybody, write the word (pause) **her.** ✔

e. (Point to **other.**) Everybody, read this word the fast way. Get ready. (Signal.) *Other.* Yes, **other.**

f. Everybody, say the sounds you write for the word (pause) **other.** Get ready. (Touch **o, th, er** as the children say:) *ooo* (pause) *th* (pause) *er.*

• (Repeat until firm.)

g. (Erase **other.**) Everybody, write the word (pause) **other.** ✔

h. (Repeat steps *e–g* for **never.**)

EXERCISE 3

Write **salt, wall, brother, went**

a. You're going to write the word (pause) **salt.** Think about the sounds in **salt** and write the word. ✔

b. (Repeat step *a* for **wall, brother, went.**)

SENTENCE WRITING
EXERCISE 4

Write two sentences

a. Listen to this sentence. **We had fun with the cow.** Say that sentence. Get ready. (Signal.) *We had fun with the cow.*

b. Now you're going to say that sentence the slow way. Get ready. (Signal for each word as the children say:) *We* (pause) *had* (pause) *fun* (pause) *with* (pause) *the* (pause) *cow.*

c. Everybody, write the sentence. Spell each word the right way. ✔

d. (Repeat steps *a–c* for **She has a bat and a ball.**)

LESSON 83

SOUND WRITING
EXERCISE 1

Write **al, th, ar**

a. Everybody, you're going to write the two letters that go together and make the sound **al.** What sound? (Signal.) *al.*

b. Write **al.** ✔

c. (Repeat steps *a* and *b* for **th** and **ar.**)

WORD WRITING
EXERCISE 2

Write sound combination words **bell, fell, tell, spell**

a. (Write on the board: **bell, fell, tell, spell.**)

b. (Point to **bell.**) Everybody, read this word the fast way. Get ready. (Signal.) *Bell.* Yes, **bell.**

c. Everybody, say the sounds you write for the word (pause) **bell.** Get ready. (Touch **b, e, ll** as the children say:) *b* (pause) *eee* (pause) *lll.*

d. (Erase **bell.**) Everybody, write the word (pause) **bell.** ✔

e. (Repeat steps *b–d* for **fell, tell,** and **spell.**)

EXERCISE 3

Write **ring, hill, them, shop**

a. You're going to write the word (pause) **ring.** Think about the sounds in **ring** and write the word. ✔

b. (Repeat step *a* for **hill, them, shop.**)

SENTENCE WRITING
EXERCISE 4

Write two sentences

a. Listen to this sentence. **He said she has a bug.** Say that sentence. Get ready. (Signal.) *He said she has a bug.*

b. Now you're going to say that sentence the slow way. Get ready. (Signal for each word as the children say:) *He* (pause) *said* (pause) *she* (pause) *has* (pause) *a* (pause) *bug.*

c. Everybody, write the sentence. Spell each word the right way. ✔

d. (Repeat steps *a–c* for **We sold a pink bag.**)

SOUND WRITING
EXERCISE 1

Write **ck, ar, sh**

a. Everybody, you're going to write the two letters that go together and make the sound **ck.** What sound? (Signal.) *ck.*

b. Write **ck.** ✔

c. (Repeat steps *a* and *b* for **ar** and **sh.**)

WORD WRITING
EXERCISE 2

Say the sounds, write **when, also, stop, of**

a. You're going to write the word (pause) **when.** Say the sounds in **when.** Get ready. (Tap for each sound as the children say:) *wh* (pause) *eee* (pause) *nnn.*

• (Repeat until firm.)

b. Everybody, write the word (pause) **when.** ✔

c. (Repeat steps *a* and *b* for **also, stop,** and **of.**)

EXERCISE 3

Write **with, sent, said, they**

a. You're going to write the word (pause) **with.** Think about the sounds in **with** and write the word. ✔

b. (Repeat step *a* for **sent, said, they.**)

SENTENCE WRITING
EXERCISE 4

Write two sentences

a. Listen to this sentence. **All old dogs must rest.** Say that sentence. Get ready. (Signal.) *All old dogs must rest.*

b. Now you're going to say that sentence the slow way. Get ready. (Signal for each word as the children say:) *All* (pause) *old* (pause) *dogs* (pause) *must* (pause) *rest.*

c. Everybody, write the sentence. Spell each word the right way. ✔

d. (Repeat steps *a–c* for **They sing and ring the bell.**)

LESSON 85

LETTER NAMES
EXERCISE 1

Name the letters **t, a, b, r, o, s**

a. (Write on the board: **t, a, b, r, o, s.**)

b. Your turn: See how many letter names you can say.

- (Point under **t.**) Get ready. (Tap.) *T.*
- (Tap under each remaining letter as the children say each name. Immediately say the correct letter name if the children make a mistake.)

c. (Give individual turns on **t, a, b, r, o, s.**)

EXERCISE 2

Spell the sounds **t, a, n**

a. When you spell a sound, you say the letter name. My turn to spell some sounds.

- The sound **t** is spelled with the letter **T.**
- The sound **aaa** is spelled with the letter **A.**
- The sound **nnn** is spelled with the letter **N.**

b. Your turn. I'll say sounds. You tell me the letter that spells each sound.

- Spell **t.** Get ready. (Signal.) *T.*
- Spell **aaa.** Get ready. (Signal.) *A.*
- Spell **nnn.** Get ready. (Signal.) *N.*

c. (Repeat step *b* until all students are firm.)

d. (Give individual turns on **t, aaa,** and **nnn.**)

WORD WRITING
EXERCISE 3

Write **come, salt, also, arm**

a. You're going to write the word (pause) **come.** Think about the sounds in **come** and write the word. ✔

b. (Repeat step *a* for **salt, also, arm.**)

SENTENCE WRITING
EXERCISE 4

Write two sentences

a. Listen to this sentence. **His cat ran up the hill.** Say that sentence. Get ready. (Signal.) *His cat ran up the hill.*

b. Now you're going to say that sentence the slow way. Get ready. (Signal for each word as the children say:) *His* (pause) *cat* (pause) *ran* (pause) *up* (pause) *the* (pause) *hill.*

c. Everybody, write the sentence. Spell each word the right way. ✔

d. (Repeat steps *a–c* for **That man met a bull.**)

LESSON 86

LETTER NAMES
EXERCISE 1

Name the letters **f, h, i, s, n, x**

a. (Write on the board: **f, h, i, s, n, x.**)

b. Your turn: See how many letter names you can say.

- (Point under **f.**) Get ready. (Tap.) *F.*
- (Tap under each remaining letter as the children say each name. Immediately say the correct letter name if the children make a mistake.)

c. (Give individual turns on **f, h, i, s, n, x.**)

EXERCISE 2

Spell the sounds **h, i, f**

a. When you spell a sound, you say the letter name. My turn to spell some sounds.

- The sound **h** is spelled with the letter **H.**
- The sound **iii** is spelled with the letter **I.**
- The sound **fff** is spelled with the letter **F.**

b. Your turn. I'll say sounds. You tell me the letter that spells each sound.
- Spell **h.** Get ready. (Signal.) *H.*
- Spell **iii.** Get ready. (Signal.) *I.*
- Spell **fff.** Get ready. (Signal.) *F.*

c. (Repeat step *b* until all students are firm.)

d. (Give individual turns on **h, iii,** and **fff.**)

WORD WRITING
EXERCISE 3

Write sound combination words **pick, lock, sack, sick**

a. (Write on the board: **pick, lock, sack, sick.**)

b. (Point to **pick.**) Everybody, read this word the fast way. Get ready. (Signal.) *Pick.* Yes, **pick.**

c. Everybody, say the sounds you write for the word (pause) **pick.** Get ready. (Touch **p, i, ck** as the children say:) *p* (pause) *iii* (pause) *k.*
- (Repeat until firm.)

d. (Erase **pick.**) Everybody, write the word (pause) **pick.** ✔

e. (Repeat steps *b–d* for **pick, lock, sack, sick.**)

SENTENCE WRITING
EXERCISE 4

Write two sentences

a. Listen to this sentence. **The man never sat on the rock.** Say that sentence. Get ready. (Signal.) *The man never sat on the rock.*

b. Now you're going to say that sentence the slow way. Get ready. (Signal for each word as the children say:) *The* (pause) *man* (pause) *never* (pause) *sat* (pause) *on* (pause) *the* (pause) *rock.*

c. Everybody, write the sentence. Spell each word the right way. ✔

d. (Repeat steps *a–c* for **The pig sat in mud.**)

LESSON 87

LETTER NAMES
EXERCISE 1

Name the letters **e, k, p, r, v, o**

a. (Write on the board: **e, k, p, r, v, o.**)

b. Your turn: See how many letter names you can say.
- (Point under **e.**) Get ready. (Tap.) *E.*
- (Tap under each remaining letter as the children say each name. Immediately say the correct letter name if the children make a mistake.)

c. (Give individual turns on **e, k, p, r, v, o.**)

EXERCISE 2

Spell the sounds **e, p, r, s, t**

a. When you spell a sound, you say the letter name. My turn to spell some sounds.
- The sound **eee** is spelled with the letter **E.**
- The sound **p** is spelled with the letter **P.**
- The sound **rrr** is spelled with the letter **R.**
- The sound **sss** is spelled with the letter **S.**
- The sound **t** is spelled with the letter **T.**

b. Your turn. I'll say sounds. You tell me the letter that spells each sound.
- Spell **eee.** Get ready. (Signal.) *E.*
- Spell **p.** Get ready. (Signal.) *P.*
- Spell **rrr.** Get ready. (Signal.) *R.*
- Spell **sss.** Get ready. (Signal.) *S.*
- Spell **t.** Get ready. (Signal.) *T.*

c. (Repeat step *b* until all students are firm.)

d. (Give individual turns on **eee, p, rrr, sss,** and **t.**)

WORD WRITING
EXERCISE 3

Write **said, other, come, wall**

a. You're going to write the word (pause) **said.** Think about the sounds in **said** and write the word. ✔

b. (Repeat step *a* for **said, other, come, wall.**)

57

EXERCISE 4

Write two sentences

a. Listen to this sentence. **The cat met the hen.** Say that sentence. Get ready. (Signal.) *The cat met the hen.*

b. Now you're going to say that sentence the slow way. Get ready. (Signal for each word as the children say:) *The* (pause) *cat* (pause) *met* (pause) *the* (pause) *hen.*

c. Everybody, write the sentence. Spell each word the right way. ✔

d. (Repeat steps *a–c* for **He sat on the bed.**)

LESSON 88

LETTER NAMES
EXERCISE 1

Name the letters **d, l, a, w, z, i**

a. (Write on the board: **d, l, a, w, z, i.**)

b. Your turn: See how many letter names you can say.

- (Point under **d.**) Get ready. (Tap.) *D.*
- (Tap under each remaining letter as the children say each name. Immediately say the correct letter name if the children make a mistake.)

c. (Give individual turns on **d, l, a, w, z, i.**)

EXERCISE 2

Spell the sounds **d, l, k, n, w**

a. When you spell a sound, you say the letter name. My turn to spell some sounds.

- The sound **d** is spelled with the letter **D.**
- The sound **lll** is spelled with the letter **L.**
- The sound **k** is spelled with the letter **K.**
- The sound **nnn** is spelled with the letter **N.**
- The sound **www** is spelled with the letter **W.**

b. Your turn. I'll say sounds. You tell me the letter that spells each sound.

- Spell **d.** Get ready. (Signal.) *D.*
- Spell **lll.** Get ready. (Signal.) *L.*
- Spell **k.** Get ready. (Signal.) *K.* (Also accept *C* or *C–K.*)
- Spell **nnn.** Get ready. (Signal.) *N.*
- Spell **www.** Get ready. (Signal.) *W.* (Also accept *W–H.*)

c. (Repeat step *b* until all students are firm.)

d. (Give individual turns on **d, lll, k, nnn,** and **www.**)

WORD WRITING
EXERCISE 3

Write **was, ring, where, ever**

a. You're going to write the word (pause) **was.** Think about the sounds in **was** and write the word. ✔

b. (Repeat step *a* for **was, ring, where, ever.**)

SENTENCE WRITING
EXERCISE 4

Write two sentences

a. Listen to this sentence. **A bad barn fell on the man.** Say that sentence. Get ready. (Signal.) *A bad barn fell on the man.*

b. Now you're going to say that sentence the slow way. Get ready. (Signal for each word as the children say:) *A* (pause) *bad* (pause) *barn* (pause) *fell* (pause) *on* (pause) *the* (pause) *man.*

c. Everybody, write the sentence. Spell each word the right way. ✔

d. (Repeat *a–c* for **This fish can swim in mud.**)

LESSON 89

LETTER NAMES
EXERCISE 1

Name the letters **j, m, a, u, y**

a. (Write on the board: **j, m, q, u, y.**)

b. Your turn: See how many letter names you can say.

• (Point under **j.**) Get ready. (Tap.) *J.*

• (Tap under each remaining letter as the children say each name. Immediately say the correct letter name if the children make a mistake.)

c. (Give individual turns on **j, m, q, u.**)

EXERCISE 2

Spell the sounds **o, b, m, r, f**

a. When you spell a sound, you say the letter name. My turn to spell some sounds.

• The sound **ooo** is spelled with the letter **O.**

• The sound **b** is spelled with the letter **B.**

• The sound **mmm** is spelled with the letter **M.**

• The sound **rrr** is spelled with the letter **R.**

• The sound **fff** is spelled with the letter **F.**

b. Your turn. I'll say sounds. You tell me the letter that spells each sound.

• Spell **ooo.** Get ready. (Signal.) *O.*

• Spell **b.** Get ready. (Signal.) *B.*

• Spell **mmm.** Get ready. (Signal.) *M.*

• Spell **rrr.** Get ready. (Signal.) *R.*

• Spell **fff.** Get ready. (Signal.) *F.*

c. (Repeat step *b* until all students are firm.)

d. (Give individual turns on **ooo, b, mmm, rrr,** and **fff.**)

WORD WRITING
EXERCISE 3

Write **they, sent, when, pick**

a. You're going to write the word (pause) **they.** Think about the sounds in **they** and write the word. ✔

b. (Repeat step *a* for **they, sent, when, pick.**)

SENTENCE WRITING
EXERCISE 4

Write two sentences

a. Listen to this sentence. **We will call the dog.** Say that sentence. Get ready. (Signal.) *We will call the dog.*

b. Now you're going to say that sentence the slow way. Get ready. (Signal for each word as the children say:) *We* (pause) *will* (pause) *call* (pause) *the* (pause) *dog.*

c. Everybody, write the sentence. Spell each word the right way. ✔

d. (Repeat steps *a–c* for **They come up the hill.**)

LESSON 90

LETTER NAMES
EXERCISE 1

Name the letters **h, n, i, f, t**

a. (Write on the board: **h, n, i, f, t.**)

b. Your turn: See how many letter names you can say.

• (Point under **h.**) Get ready. (Tap.) *H.*

• (Tap under each remaining letter as the children say each name. Immediately say the correct letter name if the children make a mistake.)

c. (Give individual turns on **h, n, i, f, t.**)

EXERCISE 2

Spell the sounds **u, s, g, d**

a. When you spell a sound, you say the letter name. My turn to spell some sounds.

• The sound **uuu** is spelled with the letter **U.**

• The sound **sss** is spelled with the letter **S.**

• The sound **g** is spelled with the letter **G.**

• The sound **d** is spelled with the letter **D.**

b. Your turn. I'll say sounds. You tell me the letter that spells each sound.

• Spell **uuu.** Get ready. (Signal.) *U.*

• Spell **sss.** Get ready. (Signal.) *S.*

• Spell **g.** Get ready. (Signal.) *G.*

• Spell **d.** Get ready. (Signal.) *D.*

c. (Repeat step *b* until all students are firm.)

d. (Give individual turns on **uuu, sss, g,** and **d.**)

WORD WRITING
EXERCISE 3

Write **never, rock, are, what**

a. You're going to write the word (pause) **never.** Think about the sounds in **never** and write the word. ✔

b. (Repeat step *a* for **rock, are, what.**)

SENTENCE WRITING
EXERCISE 4

Write two sentences

a. Listen to this sentence. **A big thing fell in the sand.**
Say that sentence. Get ready. (Signal.) *A big thing fell in the sand.*

b. Now you're going to say that sentence the slow way. Get ready. (Signal.) (Signal for each word as the children say:) *A* (pause) *big* (pause) *thing* (pause) *fell* (pause) *in* (pause) *the* (pause) *sand.*

c. Everybody, write the sentence. Spell each word the right way. ✔

d. (Repeat steps *a–c* for **A hen fell in the mud.**)

SECTION 2
Spelling by Letter Names
Lessons 91–160

LESSON 91

EXERCISE 1
LETTER NAMES

a. I'll say sounds. You tell me the **two letters** that spell each sound.

b. Spell **sh.** Get ready. (Signal.) *S-H.*

c. Spell **k.** Get ready. (Signal.) *C-K.*

d. Spell **ch.** Get ready. (Signal.) *C-H.*

e. Spell **th.** Get ready. (Signal.) *T-H.*

f. (Repeat steps *b–e* until all students are firm.)

g. (Give individual turns on **sh, ck, ch,** and **th.**)

EXERCISE 2
SAY THE SOUNDS

a. Listen: **hat.** Say it. (Signal.) *Hat.*

b. I'll say the sounds in **hat: h . . . aaa . . . t.** Say the sounds in **hat.** Get ready. (Tap for each sound.) *h . . . aaa . . . t.*

> **To Correct**
> • (Return to step *a.*)

c. What's the first sound in **hat?** (Signal.) *h.*

> **To Correct**
> • (Say the correct sound.)
> • (Return to step *a.*)

d. Next sound? (Signal.) *aaa.*

e. Next sound? (Signal.) *t.*

f. Listen: **she.** Say it. (Signal.) *She.*

g. I'll say the sounds in **she: sh . . . ēēē.**

h. Say the sounds in **she.** Get ready. (Tap for each sound.) *sh . . . ēēē.*

i. What is the first sound in **she?** (Signal.) *sh.*

j. Next sound? (Signal.) *ēēē.*

k. Yes. Those are the sounds in **she.**

• (Repeat steps *f–k* for **mat.**)

l. (Call on individual students to say the sounds in **hat, she, mat.**)

EXERCISE 3
SPELLING WORDS

a. (Write on the board:)

> 1. hot
> 2. map
> 3. he

b. Word 1 is **hot.** I'll spell **hot. H-O-T.**

• Your turn. Spell **hot.** Get ready. (Signal.) *H-O-T.*

c. Word 2 is **map.** I'll spell **map. M-A-P.**

• Your turn. Spell **map.** Get ready. (Signal.) *M-A-P.*

d. Word 3 is **he.** I'll spell **he. H-E.**

• Your turn. Spell **he.** Get ready. (Signal.) *H-E.*

e. (Give individual turns on **1. hot, 2. map, 3. he.**)

EXERCISE 4
SENTENCE WRITING

a. Listen to this sentence: **The map is red.**

b. Say that sentence. Get ready. (Signal.) *The map is red.*

c. Write the sentence. ✔

d. I'll spell each word. Check your work. Make an **X** next to any word you got wrong.

e. First word: **The. T-H-E.**

f. Next word: **map. M-A-P.**

g. (Repeat step *f* for **is, red.**)

61

LESSON 92

EXERCISE 1
WORD COMPLETION

a. (Write on the board:)

> 1. m _ t
> 2. _ an
> 3. m _

b. Copy the board. ✔
c. Word 1 is supposed to be **met.**
   What word? (Signal.) *Met.*
• Say the sounds in **met.** Get ready.
   mmm (pause) *eee* (pause) *t.*
• A letter for one of those sounds is
   missing. What sound? (Signal.) *eee.*
• Spell **eee.** Get ready. (Signal.) *E.*
• Write it in the blank.
d. Word 2 is supposed to be **tan.** What
   word? (Signal.) *Tan.*
• Say the sounds in **tan.** Get ready.
   t (pause) *aaa* (pause) *nnn.*
• A letter for one of those sounds is
   missing. What sound? (Signal.) *aaa.*
• Spell **aaa.** Get ready. (Signal.) *A.*
• Write it in the blank. ✔
e. Word 3 is supposed to be **me.** What
   word? (Signal.) *Me.*
• Say the sounds in **me.** Get ready. *mmm*
   (pause) *ēēē.*
• A letter for one of those sounds is
   missing. What sound? (Signal.) *ēēē.*
• Spell *ēēē.* Get ready. (Signal.) *E.*
• Write it in the blank. ✔
f. Get ready to spell the words you just
   wrote.
g. Look at word 1. What word? (Signal.) *Met.*
• Spell **met.** Get ready. (Signal.) *M-E-T.*
• Make sure your word is spelled **M-E-T.**
   Fix it if it's not spelled right.
h. (Repeat step *g* for **2. tan, 3. me.**)

EXERCISE 2
SAY THE SOUNDS

a. Listen: **ham.** Say it. (Signal.) *Ham.*
b. I'll say the sounds in **ham: h . . . aaa
   . . . mmm.**
• Say the sounds in **ham.** Get ready. (Tap
   for each sound.) *h . . .aaa . . . mmm.*

To Correct
• (Return to step *a*.)

c. What's the first sound in **ham?** (Signal.) *h.*

To Correct
• (Say the correct sound.)
• (Return to step *a*.)

d. Next sound? (Signal.) *aaa.*
e. Next sound? (Signal.) *mmm.*
f. Listen: **pot.** Say it. (Signal.) *Pot.*
g. I'll say the sounds in **pot: p . . . ooo
   . . . t.**
h. Say the sounds in **pot.** Get ready. (Tap
   for each sound.) *p . . . ooo . . . t.*
i. What is the first sound in **pot?** (Signal.) *p.*
j. Next sound? (Signal.) *ooo.*
k. Next sound? (Signal.) *t.*
• Yes. Those are the sounds in **pot.**
l. (Repeat steps *f–k* for **so.**)
m. (Call on individual students to say the
   sounds in **ham, pot, so.**)

EXERCISE 3
SPELLING WORDS

a. (Write on the board:)

> 1. mat
> 2. tip
> 3. she

b. Word 1 is **mat.** I'll spell **mat. M-A-T.**
• Your turn. Spell **mat.** Get ready. (Signal.)
   M-A-T.
c. Word 2 is **tip.** I'll spell **tip. T-I-P.**
• Your turn. Spell **tip.** Get ready. (Signal.)
   T-I-P.

d. Word 3 is **she.** I'll spell **she. S-H-E.**
• Your turn. Spell **she.** Get ready. (Signal.) *S-H-E.*
e. (Give individual turns on **1. mat, 2. tip 3. she.**)

EXERCISE 4
SENTENCE WRITING

a. Listen to this sentence: **The fish is wet.**
b. Say that sentence. Get ready. (Signal.) *The fish is wet.*
c. Write the sentence. ✔
d. I'll spell each word. Check your work. Make an **X** next to any word you got wrong.
e. First word: **The. T-H-E.**
f. Next word: **fish. F-I-S-H.**
g. (Repeat step *f* for **is, wet.**)

LESSON 93

EXERCISE 1
WORD COMPLETION

a. (Write on the board:)

1. f_n
2. wh_n
3. ca _d

b. Copy the board. ✔
c. Word 1 is supposed to be **fan.** What word? (Signal.) *Fan.*
• Say the sounds in **fan.** Get ready. *fff* (pause) *aaa* (pause) *nnn.*
• A letter for one of those sounds is missing. What sound? (Signal.) *aaa.*
• Spell **aaa.** Get ready. (Signal.) *A.*
• Write it in the blank. ✔
d. Word 2 is supposed to be **when.** What word? (Signal.) *When.*
• Say the sounds in **when.** Get ready. *wh* (pause) *eee* (pause) *nnn.*
• A letter for one of those sounds is missing. What sound? (Signal.) *eee.*

• Spell **eee.** Get ready. (Signal.) *E.*
• Write it in the blank. ✔
e. Word 3 is supposed to be **card.** What word? (Signal.) *Card.*
• Say the sounds in **card.** Get ready. *k* (pause) *ar* (pause) *d.*
• A letter for one of those sounds is missing. What sound? (Signal.) *r.*
• Spell **r.** Get ready. (Signal.) *R.*
• Write it in the blank. ✔
f. Get ready to spell the words you just wrote.
g. Look at word 1. What word? (Signal.) *Fan.*
• Spell **fan.** Get ready. (Signal.) *F-A-N.*
• Make sure your word is spelled **F-A-N.** Fix it if it's not spelled right.
h. (Repeat step *g* for **2. when, 3. card.**)

EXERCISE 2
SAY THE SOUNDS

a. Listen: **shop.** Say it. (Signal.) *Shop.*
b. I'll say the sounds in **shop: sh . . . ooo . . . p.** Say the sounds in **shop.** Get ready. (Tap for each sound.) *sh . . . ooo . . . p.*

To Correct
• (Return to step *a.*)

c. What's the first sound in **shop?** (Signal.) *sh.*

To Correct
• (Say the correct sound.)
• (Return to step *a.*)

d. Next sound? (Signal.) *ooo.*
e. Next sound? (Signal.) *p.*
f. Listen: **get.** Say it. (Signal.) *Get.*
g. I'll say the sounds in **get: g . . . eee . . . t.**
h. Say the sounds in **get.** Get ready. (Tap for each sound.) *g . . . eee . . . t.*
i. What is the first sound in **get?** (Signal.) *g.*
j. Next sound? (Signal.) *eee.*
k. Next sound? (Signal.) *t.*
• Yes. Those are the sounds in **get.**
• (Repeat steps *f–k* for **and.**)
l. (Call on individual students to say the sounds in: **shop, get, and.**)

63

EXERCISE 3
SPELLING WORDS

a. (Write on the board:)

> 1. so
> 2. me
> 3. stop

b. Word 1 is **so.** I'll spell **so. S-O.**
• Your turn. Spell **so.** Get ready. (Signal.) *S-O.*
c. Word 2 is **me.** I'll spell **me. M-E.**
• Your turn. Spell **me.** Get ready. (Signal.) *M-E.*
d. Word 3 is **stop.** I'll spell **stop. S-T-O-P.**
• Your turn. Spell **stop.** Get ready. (Signal.) *S-T-O-P.*
e. (Give individual turns on **1. so, 2. me, 3. stop.**)

EXERCISE 4
SENTENCE WRITING

a. Listen to this sentence: **We fed the dog.**
b. Say that sentence. Get ready. (Signal.) *We fed the dog.*
c. Write the sentence. ✔
d. I'll spell each word. Check your work. Make an **X** next to any word you got wrong.
e. First word: **We. W-E.**
f. Next word: **fed. F-E-D.**
g. (Repeat step *f* for **the, dog.**)

LESSON 94

EXERCISE 1
LETTER SOUNDS

a. Everybody, you're going to write the two letters that go together and make the sound **er.** What sound? (Signal.) *er.*
b. Write **er.** ✔
c. What letters did you write? (Signal.) *E-R.*
d. (Repeat steps *a–c* for **al** and **ck.**)

EXERCISE 2
SAY THE SOUNDS

a. Listen: **set.** Say it. (Signal.) *Set.*
b. I'll say the sounds in **set: sss . . . eee . . . t.**
• Say the sounds in **set.** Get ready. (Tap for each sound.) *sss . . . eee . . . t.*

To Correct ─────
• (Return to step *a.*)

c. What's the first sound in **set?** (Signal.) *sss.*

To Correct ─────
• (Say the correct sound.)
• (Return to step *a.*)

d. Next sound? (Signal.) *eee.*
e. Next sound? (Signal.) *t.*
f. Listen: **cap.** Say it. (Signal.) *Cap.*
g. I'll say the sounds in **cap: k . . . aaa . . . p.**
h. Say the sounds in **cap.** Get ready. (Tap for each sound.) *k . . . aaa . . . p.*
i. What is the first sound in **cap?** (Signal.) *k.*
j. Next sound? (Signal.) *aaa.*
k. Next sound? (Signal.) *p.*
Yes. Those are the sounds in **cap.**
• (Repeat steps *f–k* for **swim.**)
l. (Call on individual students to say the sounds in **set, cap, swim.**)

EXERCISE 3
SPELLING WORDS

a. (Write on the board:)

> 1. and
> 2. mop
> 3. pig
> 4. what

b. Word 1 is **and.** Spell **and.** Get ready. (Signal.) *A-N-D.*
c. Word 2 is **mop.** Spell **mop.** Get ready. (Signal.) *M-O-P.*

64

d. (Repeat step c for **3. pig, 4. what.**)
e. (Give individual turns on **1. and,
    2. mop, 3. pig, 4. what.**)

EXERCISE 4
SENTENCE WRITING

a. Listen to this sentence: **She did not bet.**
b. Say that sentence. Get ready. (Signal.)
   She did not bet.
c. Write the sentence. ✔
d. I'll spell each word. Check your work.
   Make an **X** next to any word you got
   wrong.
e. First word: **She. S-H-E.**
f. Next word: **did. D-I-D.**
g. (Repeat step f for **not, bet.**)

LESSON 95

EXERCISE 1
WORD COMPLETION

a. (Write on the board:)

> 1. an_
> 2. _ed
> 3. d_g

b. Copy the board. ✔
c. Word 1 is supposed to be **and.**
   What word? (Signal.) *And.*
• A letter is missing for **and.**
   What letter? (Signal.) *D.*
• Write it in the blank. ✔
d. Word 2 is supposed to be **bed.**
   What word? (Signal.) *Bed.*
• A letter is missing for **bed.**
   What letter? (Signal.) *B.*
• Write it in the blank. ✔
e. Word 3 is supposed to be **dog.**
   What word? (Signal.) *Dog.*
• A letter is missing for **dog.**
   What letter? (Signal.) *O.*
• Write it in the blank. ✔
f. Get ready to spell the words you just
   wrote.

g. Look at word 1.
   What word? (Signal.) *And.*
• Spell **and.** Get ready. (Signal.) *A-N-D.*
• Fix it if it's not spelled right.
h. (Repeat step g for **2. bed, 3. dog.**)

EXERCISE 2
SPELLING WORDS

a. (Write on the board:)

> 1. salt
> 2. said
> 3. was
> 4. ship

b. Word 1 is **salt.** Spell **salt.** Get ready.
   (Signal.) *S-A-L-T.*
c. Word 2 is **said.** Spell **said.** Get ready.
   (Signal.) *S-A-I-D.*
d. (Repeat step c for **3. was, 4. ship.**)
e. (Give individual turns on **1. salt,
    2. said, 3. was, 4. ship.**)

EXERCISE 3
SPELLING REVIEW

a. Get ready to spell and write some words.
b. Word 1 is **met.** What word? (Signal.) *Met.*
• Spell **met.** Get ready. (Signal.) *M-E-T.*
• Write it. ✔
c. Word 2 is **when.** What word? (Signal.)
   When.
• Spell **when.** Get ready. (Signal.) *W-H-E-N.*
• Write it. ✔
d. (Repeat step c for **3. at, 4. sand.**)
e. I'll spell each word.
• Put an **X** next to any word you missed
   and write that word correctly.
• (Spell each word twice. Write the words
   on the board as you spell them.)

LESSON 96

EXERCISE 1
SAY THE SOUNDS

a. Listen: **bag.** Say it. (Signal.) *Bag.*

b. What's the first sound in **bag?** (Signal.) *b.*

To Correct
- Listen: **b . . . aaa . . . g.**
- (Repeat step *b.*)

c. Next sound? (Signal.) *aaa.*
d. Next sound? (Signal.) *g.*
Yes. Those are the sounds in **bag.**
e. (Repeat steps *a–d* for **he, sack.**)
f. (Call on individual students to say the sounds in **bag, he, sack.**)

EXERCISE 2
SPELLING WORDS

a. (Write on the board:)

1. there
2. has
3. fish
4. come

b. Word 1 is **there.** Spell **there.** Get ready. (Signal.) *T-H-E-R-E.*
c. Word 2 is **has.** Spell **has.** Get ready. (Signal.) *H-A-S.*
d. (Repeat step *c* for **3. fish, 4. come.**)
e. (Give individual turns on **1. there, 2. has, 3. fish, 4. come.**)

EXERCISE 3
SPELLING REVIEW

a. Get ready to spell and write some words.
b. Word 1 is **said.** What word? (Signal.) *Said.*
- Spell **said.** Get ready. (Signal.) *S-A-I-D.*
- Write it. ✔
c. Word 2 is **was.** What word? (Signal.) *Was.*
- Spell **was.** Get ready. (Signal.) *W-A-S.*
- Write it. ✔
d. (Repeat step *c* for **3. what, 4. mop.**)
e. I'll spell each word.
- Put an **X** next to any word you missed and write that word correctly.
- (Spell each word twice. Write the words on the board as you spell them.)

LESSON 97

EXERCISE 1
WORD COMPLETION

a. (Write on the board:)

1. _ap
2. h_t
3. sh_t

b. Copy the board. ✔
c. Word 1 is supposed to be **cap.** What word? (Signal.) *Cap.*
- A letter is missing for **cap.** What letter? (Signal.) *C.*
- Write it in the blank. ✔
d. Word 2 is supposed to be **hut.** What word? (Signal.) *Hut.*
- A letter is missing for **hut.** What letter? (Signal.) *U.*
- Write it in the blank. ✔
e. Word 3 is supposed to be **shot.** What word? (Signal.) *Shot.*
- A letter is missing for **shot.** What letter? (Signal.) *O.*
- Write it in the blank. ✔
f. Get ready to spell the words you just wrote.
g. Look at word 1. What word? (Signal.) *Cap.*
- Spell **cap.** Get ready. (Signal.) *C-A-P.*
- Fix it if it's not spelled right.
h. (Repeat step *g* for **2. hut, 3. shot.**)

EXERCISE 2
SENTENCE COPYING

Children are responsible for copying capital letters.

a. (Write on the board:)

What are we to do?

- I'll read the sentence on the board: **What are we to do?**

b. Spell **What.** Get ready. (Signal.) *W-H-A-T.*
• Spell **are.** Get ready. (Signal.) *A-R-E.*
• Spell **we.** Get ready. (Signal.) *W-E.*
• Spell **to.** Get ready. (Signal.) *T-O.*
• Spell **do.** Get ready. (Signal.) *D-O.*
c. Copy this sentence on lined paper.
d. (Pause, then check and correct.)
• Read the sentence you just copied. Get ready. (Signal.) *What are we to do?*

EXERCISE 3
SPELLING REVIEW

a. Get ready to spell and write some words.
b. Word 1 is **stop.** What word? (Signal.) *Stop.*
• Spell **stop.** Get ready. (Signal.) *S-T-O-P.*
• Write it. ✔
c. Word 2 is **swim.** What word? (Signal.) *Swim.*
• Spell **swim.** Get ready. (Signal.) *S-W-I-M.*
• Write it. ✔
d. (Repeat step *c* for **3. ran, 4. wish.**)
e. I'll spell each word.
• Put an **X** next to any word you missed and write that word correctly.
• (Spell each word twice. Write the words on the board as you spell them.)

LESSON 98

EXERCISE 1
SAY THE SOUNDS

a. Listen: **this.** Say it. (Signal.) *This.*
b. What's the first sound in **this?** (Signal.) *th.*

┌─ **To Correct** ──────────────┐
│ • Listen: **th . . . iii . . . sss.** │
│ • (Repeat step *b.*) │
└──────────────────────────────┘

c. Next sound? (Signal.) *iii.*
d. Next sound? (Signal.) *sss.*
   Yes. Those are the sounds in **this.**
e. (Repeat steps *a–d* for **back, ring.**)
f. (Call on individual students to say the sounds in **this, back, ring.**)

EXERCISE 2
SENTENCE REVIEW

a. (Write on the board:)

> **What are we to do?**

• I'll read the sentence on the board: **What are we to do?**
b. Spell **What.** Get ready. (Signal.) *W-H-A-T.*
• Spell **are.** Get ready. (Signal.) *A-R-E.*
• Spell **we.** Get ready. (Signal.) *W-E.*
• Spell **to.** Get ready. (Signal.) *T-O.*
• Spell **do.** Get ready. (Signal.) *D-O.*
c. (Erase the board.)
d. Now let's spell the words in that sentence without looking.
• Spell **What.** Get ready. (Signal.) *W-H-A-T.*
• Spell **are.** Get ready. (Signal.) *A-R-E.*
• Spell **we.** Get ready. (Signal.) *W-E.*
• Spell **to.** Get ready. (Signal.) *T-O.*
• Spell **do.** Get ready. (Signal.) *D-O.*

EXERCISE 3
SPELLING REVIEW

a. Get ready to spell and write some words.
b. Word 1 is **said.** What word? (Signal.) *Said.*
• Spell **said.** Get ready. (Signal.) *S-A-I-D.*
• Write it. ✔
c. Word 2 is **what.** What word? (Signal.) *What.*
• Spell **what.** Get ready. (Signal.) *W-H-A-T.*
• Write it. ✔
d. (Repeat step *c* for **3. this, 4. barn.**)
e. I'll spell each word.
• Put an **X** next to any word you missed and write that word correctly.
• (Spell each word twice. Write the words on the board as you spell them.)

LESSON 99

EXERCISE 1
IDENTIFYING SPELLED WORDS

a. I'll spell **hat** and **me.**
b. What words? (Signal.) *Hat and me.*

c. Listen to this word: **M-E.**
- Listen again: **M-E.**
- What word? (Signal.) *Me.*

d. Listen to this word: **H-A-T.**
- Listen again: **H-A-T.**
- What word? (Signal.) *Hat.*

EXERCISE 2
SENTENCE COMPLETION

a. (Write on the board:)

> Wh _ t ar _ w _ t _ d _?

- The sentence should say: **What are we to do?**

b. Write that sentence on lined paper. Fill in the blanks. ✔

c. Now let's spell those words without looking.
- Spell **What.** Get ready. (Signal.) *W-H-A-T.*
- Spell **are.** Get ready. (Signal.) *A-R-E.*
- Spell **we.** Get ready. (Signal.) *W-E.*
- Spell **to.** Get ready. (Signal.) *T-O.*
- Spell **do.** Get ready. (Signal.) *D-O.*

d. (Write to show:)

> What are we to do?

e. Fix any words you missed. ✔

EXERCISE 3
SPELLING REVIEW

a. Get ready to spell and write some words.

b. Word 1 is **when.** What word? (Signal.) *When.*
- Spell **when.** Get ready. (Signal.) *W-H-E-N.*
- Write it. ✔

c. Word 2 is **them.** What word? (Signal.) *Them.*
- Spell **them.** Get ready. (Signal.) *T-H-E-M.*
- Write it. ✔

d. (Repeat step *c* for **3. farm, 4. stop.**)

e. I'll spell each word.
- Put an **X** next to any word you missed and write that word correctly.
- (Spell each word twice. Write the words on the board as you spell them.)

LESSON 100

EXERCISE 1
IDENTIFYING SPELLED WORDS

a. I'll spell **top** and **hat.**

b. What words? (Signal.) *Top and hat.*

c. Listen to this word: **T-O-P.**
- Listen again: **T-O-P.**
- What word? (Signal.) *Top.*

d. Listen to this word: **H-A-T.**
- Listen again: **H-A-T.**
- What word? (Signal.) *Hat.*

EXERCISE 2
SENTENCE COMPLETION

a. (Write on the board:)

> W _ _ t _re _ _ _ _ _ _?

- The sentence should say: **What are we to do?**

b. Write that sentence on lined paper. Fill in the blanks. ✔

c. Now let's spell those words without looking.
- Spell **What.** Get ready. (Signal.) *W-H-A-T.*
- Spell **are.** Get ready. (Signal.) *A-R-E.*
- Spell **we.** Get ready. (Signal.) *W-E.*
- Spell **to.** Get ready. (Signal.) *T-O.*
- Spell **do.** Get ready. (Signal.) *D-O.*

d. (Write to show:)

> What are we to do?

e. Fix any words you missed. ✔

EXERCISE 3
SPELLING REVIEW

a. Get ready to spell and write some words.

b. Word 1 is **was.** What word? (Signal.) *Was.*
- Spell **was.** Get ready. (Signal.) *W-A-S.*
- Write it. ✔

c. Word 2 is **sand.** What word? (Signal.) *Sand.*
- Spell **sand.** Get ready. (Signal.) *S-A-N-D.*
- Write it. ✔

d. (Repeat step *c* for **when.**)

e. I'll spell each word.
- Put an **X** next to any word you missed and write that word correctly.
- (Spell each word twice. Write the words on the board as you spell them: **1. was, 2. sand, 3. when.**)

LESSON 101

EXERCISE 1
IDENTIFYING SPELLED WORDS

a. I'll spell some words. See if you can tell which word I spell.

b. Listen to this word: **M-O-P.**
- Listen again: **M-O-P.**
- What word? (Signal.) *Mop.*

c. Listen to this word: **H-E.**
- Listen again: **H-E.**
- What word? (Signal.) *He.*

d. (Repeat step *c* for **am.**)

EXERCISE 2
SENTENCE COMPLETION

a. (Write on the board:)

> _ _ _ _ _ _ e w_ _ _ _ _?

- The sentence should say: **What are we to do?**

b. Write that sentence on lined paper. Fill in the blanks. ✔

c. Now let's spell those words without looking.
- Spell **What.** Get ready. (Signal.) *W-H-A-T.*
- Spell **are.** Get ready. (Signal.) *A-R-E.*
- Spell **we.** Get ready. (Signal.) *W-E.*
- Spell **to.** Get ready. (Signal.) *T-O.*
- Spell **do.** Get ready. (Signal.) *D-O.*

d. (Write to show:)

> What are we to do?

e. Fix any words you missed. ✔

EXERCISE 3
SPELLING REVIEW

a. Get ready to spell and write some words.

b. Word 1 is **there.** What word? (Signal.) *There.*
- Spell **there.** Get ready. (Signal.) *T-H-E-R-E.*
- Write it. ✔

c. Word 2 is **said.** What word? (Signal.) *Said.*
- Spell **said.** Get ready. (Signal.) *S-A-I-D.*
- Write it. ✔

d. (Repeat step *c* for **3. pig, 4. fish.**)

e. I'll spell each word.
- Put an **X** next to any word you missed and write that word correctly.
- (Spell each word twice. Write the words on the board as you spell them.)

LESSON 102

EXERCISE 1
PATTERNS

a. (Write on the board:)

> 1. rich
> 2. chin
> 3. such
> 4. chop

- These words have the sound **ch.**

b. Word 1 is **rich.** Spell **rich.** Get ready. (Signal.) *R-I-C-H.*

c. Word 2 is **chin.** Spell **chin.** Get ready. (Signal.) *C-H-I-N.*

d. (Repeat step *c* for **3. such, 4. chop.**)

e. (Give individual turns on **1. rich, 2. chin, 3. such, 4. chop.**)

EXERCISE 2
SENTENCE WRITING

a. You're going to write this sentence: **What are we to do?**

b. Say the sentence. Get ready. (Signal.) *What are we to do?*

c. Write the sentence. ✔
d. (Write on the board:)

> **What are we to do?**

e. Check your work. Make an **X** next to any word you got wrong.
f. Word 1. Spell **What.** Get ready. (Tap for each letter.) *W-H-A-T.*
• (Repeat for **are, we, to, do.**)

EXERCISE 3
SPELLING REVIEW

a. Get ready to spell and write some words.
b. Word 1 is **has.**
• What word? (Signal.) *Has.*
• Spell **has.** Get ready. (Signal.) *H-A-S.*
• Write it. ✔
c. Word 2 is **farm.**
• What word? (Signal.) *Farm.*
• Spell **farm.** Get ready. (Signal.) *F-A-R-M.*
• Write it. ✔
d. (Repeat step *c* for **3. she, 4. this.**)
e. I'll spell each word.
• Put an **X** next to any word you missed and write that word correctly.
• (Spell each word twice. Write the words on the board as you spell them.)

LESSON **103**

EXERCISE 1
PATTERNS

a. (Write on the board:)

> 1. lunch
> 2. inch
> 3. chin
> 4. charm

These words have the sound **ch.**
b. Word 1 is **lunch.** Spell **lunch.** Get ready. (Signal.) *L-U-N-C-H.*
c. Word 2 is **inch.** Spell **inch.** Get ready. (Signal.) *I-N-C-H.*
d. (Repeat step *c* for **3. chin, 4. charm.**)

e. (Give individual turns on: **1. lunch, 2. inch, 3. chin, 4. charm.**)

EXERCISE 2
SPELLING WORDS

a. (Write on the board:)

> 1. back
> 2. ball
> 3. now
> 4. where

b. Word 1 is **back.** Spell **back.** Get ready. (Signal.) *B-A-C-K.*
c. Word 2 is **ball.** Spell **ball.** Get ready. (Signal.) *B-A-L-L.*
d. (Repeat step *c* for **3. now, 4. where.**)
• (Erase the board.)
e. Spell those words without looking.
f. Word 1 is **back.** Spell **back.** Get ready. (Signal.) *B-A-C-K.*
g. Word 2 is **ball.** Spell **ball.** Get ready. (Signal.) *B-A-L-L.*
h. (Repeat step *g* for **3. now, 4. where.**)

EXERCISE 3
SPELLING REVIEW

a. Get ready to spell and write some words.
b. Word 1 is **come.** What word? (Signal.) *Come.*
• Spell **come.** Get ready. (Signal.) *C-O-M-E.*
• Write it. ✔
c. Word 2 is **wish.** What word? (Signal.) *Wish.*
• Spell **wish.** Get ready. (Signal.) *W-I-S-H.*
• Write it. ✔
d. (Repeat step *c* for **3. are, 4. tall.**)
e. I'll spell each word.
• Put an **X** next to any word you missed and write that word correctly.
• (Spell each word twice. Write the words on the board as you spell them.)

LESSON 104

EXERCISE 1
IDENTIFYING SPELLED WORDS

a. I'll spell some words. See if you can tell which word I spell.

b. Listen to this word: **M-A-P.**
• Listen again: **M-A-P.**
• What word? (Signal.) *Map.*

c. Listen to this word: **H-O-T.**
• Listen again: **H-O-T.**
• What word? (Signal.) *Hot.*

d. (Repeat step c for **me.**)

EXERCISE 2
SPELLING WORDS

a. (Write on the board:)

> 1. on
> 2. are
> 3. was
> 4. barn

b. Word 1 is **on.** Spell **on.** Get ready. (Signal.) *O-N.*

c. Word 2 is **are.** Spell **are.** Get ready. (Signal.) *A-R-E.*

d. (Repeat step c for **3. was, 4. barn.**)
• (Erase the board.)

e. Spell those words without looking.

f. Word 1 is **on.** Spell **on.** Get ready. (Signal.) *O-N.*

g. Word 2 is **are.** Spell **are.** Get ready. (Signal.) *A-R-E.*

h. (Repeat step g for **3. was, 4. barn.**)

EXERCISE 3
SPELLING REVIEW

a. Get ready to spell and write some words.

b. Word 1 is **farm.** What word? (Signal.) *Farm.*
• Spell **farm.** Get ready. (Signal.) *F-A-R-M.*
• Write it. ✔

c. Word 2 is **call.** What word? (Signal.) *Call.*
• Spell **call.** Get ready. (Signal.) *C-A-L-L.*
• Write it. ✔

d. (Repeat step c for **3. big, 4. sing.**)

e. I'll spell each word.
• Put an **X** next to any word you missed and write that word correctly.
• (Spell each word twice. Write the words on the board as you spell them.)

LESSON 105

EXERCISE 1
WORD COMPLETION

a. (Write on the board:)

> 1. _ _ op
> 2. _ all
> 3. sa_t
> 4. f _ _ m

b. Copy the board. ✔

c. One or more letters are missing from these words. You're going to write the missing letters.

d. Word 1 is supposed to be **shop.**
• What word? (Signal.) *Shop.*
• Fill in the blanks so that the word spells **shop.**

e. Word 2 is supposed to be **mall.**
• What word? (Signal.) *Mall.*
• Fill in the blanks so that the word spells **mall.**

f. (Repeat step d for **3. salt, 4. farm.**)

g. Get ready to spell the words you just wrote.

h. Look at word 1.
• What word? (Signal.) *Shop.*
• Spell **shop.** Get ready. (Signal.) *S-H-O-P.*
• Fix it if it's not spelled right.

i. (Repeat step h for **2. mall, 3. salt, 4. farm.**)

EXERCISE 2
SPELLING WORDS

a. (Write on the board:)

> 1. was
> 2. what
> 3. march
> 4. fall

b. Word 1 is **was.** Spell **was.** Get ready. (Signal.) *W-A-S.*

c. Word 2 is **what.** Spell **what.** Get ready. (Signal.) *W-H-A-T.*

d. (Repeat step c for **3. march, 4. fall.**)

• (Erase the board.)

e. Spell those words without looking.

f. Word 1 is **was.** Spell **was.** Get ready. (Signal.) *W-A-S.*

g. Word 2 is **what.** Spell **what.** Get ready. (Signal.) *W-H-A-T.*

h. (Repeat step g for **3. march, 4. fall.**)

EXERCISE 3
SPELLING REVIEW

a. Get ready to spell and write some words.

b. Word 1 is **we.** What word? (Signal.) *We.* Spell **we.** Get ready. (Signal.) *W-E.*

• Write it. ✔

c. Word 2 is **where.** What word? (Signal.) *Where.*

• Spell **where.** Get ready. (Signal.) *W-H-E-R-E.*

• Write it. ✔

d. (Repeat step c for **3. are, 4. do.**)

e. I'll spell each word.

• Put an **X** next to any word you missed and write that word correctly.

• (Spell each word twice. Write the words on the board as you spell them.)

LESSON 106

EXERCISE 1
SAY THE SOUNDS

a. Listen: **inch.** Say it. (Signal.) *Inch.*

b. What's the first sound in **inch?** (Signal.) *iii.*

> **To Correct**
> • Listen: **iii . . . nnn . . . ch.**
> • (Repeat step *b.*)

c. Next sound? (Signal.) *nnn.*

d. Next sound? (Signal.) *ch.* Yes. Those are the sounds in **inch.**

e. (Repeat steps *a–d* for **we, stop, ball.**)

f. (Call on individual students to say the sounds in **inch, we, stop, ball.**)

EXERCISE 2
SPELLING WORDS

a. (Write on the board:)

> 1. tall
> 2. farm
> 3. his
> 4. chip

b. Word 1 is **tall.** Spell **tall.** Get ready. (Signal.) *T-A-L-L.*

c. Word 2 is **farm.** Spell **farm.** Get ready. (Signal.) *F-A-R-M.*

d. (Repeat step c for **3. his, 4. chip.**)

• (Erase the board.)

e. Spell those words without looking.

f. Word 1 is **tall.** Spell **tall.** Get ready. (Signal.) *T-A-L-L.*

g. Word 2 is **farm.** Spell **farm.** Get ready. (Signal.) *F-A-R-M.*

h. (Repeat step g for **3. now, 4. where.**)

EXERCISE 3
SPELLING REVIEW

a. Get ready to spell and write some words.

b. Word 1 is **charm.** What word? (Signal.) *Charm.*

• Spell **charm.** Get ready. (Signal.) *C-H-A-R-M.*

• Write it. ✔

c. Word 2 is **what.** What word? (Signal.) *What.*

• Spell **what.** Get ready. (Signal.) *W-H-A-T.*

• Write it. ✔

d. (Repeat step c for **3. sack, 4. bell.**)

e. I'll spell each word.
- Put an **X** next to any word you missed and write that word correctly.
- (Spell each word twice. Write the words on the board as you spell them:
  1. charm, 2. what, 3. sack, 4. bell.)

LESSON 107

EXERCISE 1
IDENTIFYING SPELLED WORDS

a. I'll spell some words.
- See if you can tell which word I spell.

b. Listen to this word: **S-O.**
- Listen again: **S-O.**
- What word? (Signal.) *So.*

c. Listen to this word: **M-A-P.**
- Listen again: **M-A-P.**
- What word? (Signal.) *Map.*

d. (Repeat step *c* for **mop.**)

EXERCISE 2
PATTERNS

a. (Write on the board:)

1. hat	4. tap
2. mad	5. ham
3. sad	6. pad

- All these words have an **aaa** sound that is spelled with the letter **A.**
- Look at the words and spell them. Then I'll call on individual students to spell them without looking.

b. Word 1: **hat.** Spell **hat.** Get ready. (Signal.) *H-A-T.*

c. Word 2: **mad.** Spell **mad.** Get ready. (Signal.) *M-A-D.*

d. (Repeat step *c* for **3. sad, 4. tap, 5. ham, 6. pad.**)

e. (Erase the board.)

f. (Call on a student.) Spell **hat.** *H-A-T.*

g. (Call on another student.) Spell **mad.** *M-A-D.*

h. (Repeat step *g* for **3. sad, 4. tap, 5. ham, 6. pad.**)

EXERCISE 3
SPELLING REVIEW

a. Get ready to spell and write some words.

b. Word 1 is **farm.** What word? (Signal.) *Farm.*
- Spell **farm.** Get ready. (Signal.) *F-A-R-M.*
- Write it. ✔

c. Word 2 is **inch.** What word? (Signal.) *Inch.*
- Spell **inch.** Get ready. (Signal.) *I-N-C-H.*
- Write it. ✔

d. (Repeat step *c* for **3. chop, 4. march.**)

e. I'll spell each word.
- Put an **X** next to any word you missed and write that word correctly.
- (Spell each word twice. Write the words on the board as you spell them.)

LESSON 108

EXERCISE 1
IDENTIFYING SPELLED WORDS

a. I'll spell some words. See if you can tell which word I spell.

b. Listen to this word: **M-O-P.**
- Listen again: **M-O-P.**
- What word? (Signal.) *Mop.*

c. Listen to this word: **T-O-P.**
- Listen again: **T-O-P.**
- What word? (Signal.) *Top.*

d. (Repeat step *c* for **hot.**)

EXERCISE 2
PATTERNS

a. (Write on the board:)

1. glad	4. ham
2. sap	5. dad
3. mat	6. pan

- All these words have an **aaa** sound that is spelled with the letter **A.**
- Look at the words and spell them. Then I'll call on individual students to spell them without looking.

b. Word 1: **glad.** Spell **glad.** Get ready. (Signal.) *G-L-A-D.*

c. Word 2: **sap.** Spell **sap.** Get ready. (Signal.) *S-A-P.*

d. (Repeat step c for **3. mat, 4. ham, 5. dad, 6. pan.**)

e. (Erase the board.)

f. (Call on a student.) Spell **glad.** *G-L-A-D.*

g. (Call on another student.) Spell **sap.** *S-A-P.*

h. (Repeat step g for **3. mat, 4. ham, 5. dad, 6. pan.**)

EXERCISE 3
SPELLING REVIEW

a. Get ready to spell and write some words.

b. Word 1 is **to.** What word? (Signal.) *To.*

• Spell **to.** Get ready. (Signal.) *T-O.*

• Write it. ✔

c. Word 2 is **where.** What word? (Signal.) *Where.*

• Spell **where.** Get ready. (Signal.) *W-H-E-R-E.*

• Write it. ✔

d. (Repeat step c for **3. map, 4. when.**)

e. I'll spell each word.

• Put an **X** next to any word you missed and write that word correctly.

• (Spell each word twice. Write the words on the board as you spell them.)

LESSON 109

EXERCISE 1
WORD COMPLETION

a. (Write on the board:)

> 1. p _ d
> 2. _ _ op
> 3. c _ _ l

b. Copy the board. ✔

c. One or more letters are missing from these words. You're going to write the missing letters.

d. Word 1 is supposed to be **pad.** What word? (Signal.) *Pad.*

• Fill in the blanks so that the word spells **pad.**

e. Word 2 is supposed to be **shop.** What word? (Signal.) *Shop.*

• Fill in the blanks so that the word spells **shop.**

f. (Repeat step d for **3. call.**)

g. Get ready to spell the words you just wrote.

h. Look at word 1. What word? (Signal.) *Pad.*

• Spell **pad.** Get ready. (Signal.) *P-A-D.*

• Fix it if it's not spelled right.

i. (Repeat step h for **2. shop, 3. call.**)

EXERCISE 2
SPELLING WORDS

a. (Write on the board:)

> 1. lunch
> 2. they
> 3. said
> 4. swim

b. Word 1 is **lunch.** Spell **lunch.** Get ready. (Signal.) *L-U-N-C-H.*

c. Word 2 is **they.** Spell **they.** Get ready. (Signal.) *T-H-E-Y.*

d. (Repeat step c for **3. said, 4. swim.**)

• (Erase the board.)

e. Spell those words without looking.

f. Word 1 is **lunch.** Spell **lunch.** Get ready. (Signal.) *L-U-N-C-H.*

g. Word 2 is **they.** Spell **they.** Get ready. (Signal.) *T-H-E-Y.*

h. (Repeat step g for **3. said, 4. swim.**)

EXERCISE 3
SPELLING REVIEW

a. Get ready to spell and write some words.

b. Word 1 is **sad.** What word? (Signal.) *Sad.*

• Spell **sad.** Get ready. (Signal.) *S-A-D.*

• Write it. ✔

74

c. Word 2 is **are.** What word? (Signal.) *Are.*
- Spell **are.** Get ready. (Signal.) *A-R-E.*
- Write it. ✔
d. (Repeat step *c* for **3. his, 4. glad.**)
e. I'll spell each word.
- Put an **X** next to any word you missed and write that word correctly.
- (Spell each word twice. Write the words on the board as you spell them.)

LESSON 110

EXERCISE 1
SAY THE SOUNDS

a. Listen: **farm.** Say it. (Signal.) *Farm.*
b. What's the first sound in **farm?** (Signal.) *fff.*

> ### To Correct
> - Listen: **fff . . . ar . . . mmm.**
> - (Repeat step *b*.)

c. Next sound? (Signal.) *ar.*
d. Next sound? (Signal.) *mmm.*
   Yes. Those are the sounds in **farm.**
e. (Repeat steps *a–d* for **lunch, shop.**)
f. (Call on individual students to say the sounds in **farm, lunch, shop.**)

EXERCISE 2
PATTERNS

a. (Write on the board:)

1. ash	4. mash
2. dash	5. hand
3. and	

- All these words have an **aaa** sound that is spelled with the letter **A.**
- Look at the words and spell them. Then I'll call on individual students to spell them without looking.
b. Word 1: **ash.** Spell **ash.** Get ready. (Signal.) *A-S-H.*

c. Word 2: **dash.** Spell **dash.** Get ready. (Signal.) *D-A-S-H.*
d. (Repeat step *c* for **3. and, 4. mash, 5. hand.**)
e. (Erase the board.)
f. (Call on a student.) Spell **ash.** *A-S-H.*
g. (Call on another student.) Spell **dash.** *D-A-S-H.*
h. (Repeat step *g* for **3. and, 4. mash, 5. hand.**)

EXERCISE 3
SPELLING REVIEW

a. Get ready to spell and write some words.
b. Word 1 is **lunch.** What word? (Signal.) *Lunch.*
- Spell **lunch.** Get ready. (Signal.) *L-U-N-C-H.*
- Write it. ✔
c. Word 2 is **them.** What word? (Signal.) *Them.*
- Spell **them.** Get ready. (Signal.) *T-H-E-M.*
- Write it. ✔
d. (Repeat step *c* for **3. said, 4. hall.**)
e. I'll spell each word.
- Put an **X** next to any word you missed and write that word correctly.
- (Spell each word twice. Write the words on the board as you spell them.)

LESSON 111

EXERCISE 1
IDENTIFYING SPELLED WORDS

a. I'll spell some words. See if you can tell which word I spell.
b. Listen to this word: **A-N-D.**
- Listen again: **A-N-D.**
- What word? (Signal.) *And.*
c. Listen to this word: **H-A-N-D.**
- Listen again: **H-A-N-D.**
- What word? (Signal.) *Hand.*
d. (Repeat step *c* for **hop.**)

EXERCISE 2
PATTERNS

a. (Write on the board:)

1. rot	4. pop
2. shop	5. dot
3. hot	6. pot

- All these words have an **ooo** sound that is spelled with the letter **O**.
- Look at the words and spell them. Then I'll call on individual students to spell them without looking.

b. Word 1: **rot.** Spell **rot.** Get ready. (Signal.) *R-O-T.*

c. Word 2: **shop.** Spell **shop.** Get ready. (Signal.) *S-H-O-P.*

d. (Repeat step *c* for **3. hot, 4. pop, 5. dot, 6. pot.**)

e. (Erase the board.)

f. (Call on a student.) Spell **pop.** *P-O-P.*

g. (Call on another student.) Spell **hot.** *H-O-T.*

h. (Repeat step *g* for **3. hot, 4. pop, 5. dot, 6. pot.**)

EXERCISE 3
SPELLING REVIEW

a. Get ready to spell and write some words.

b. Word 1 is **call.** What word? (Signal.) *Call.*
- Spell **call.** Get ready. (Signal.) *C-A-L-L.*
- Write it. ✔

c. Word 2 is **glad.** What word? (Signal.) *Glad.*
- Spell **glad.** Get ready. (Signal.) *G-L-A-D.*
- Write it. ✔

d. (Repeat step *c* for **3. barn, 4. do.**)

e. I'll spell each word.
- Put an **X** next to any word you missed and write that word correctly.
- (Spell each word twice. Write the words on the board as you spell them.)

LESSON 112

EXERCISE 1
WORD COMPLETION

a. (Write on the board:)

1. mar_ _
2. ar_
3. s_ id
4. _ _ op

b. Copy the board. ✔

c. One or more letters are missing from these words.
   You're going to write the missing letters.

d. Word 1 is supposed to be **march.**
- What word? (Signal.) *March.*
- Fill in the blanks so that the word spells **march.**

e. Word 2 is supposed to be **are.**
   What word? (Signal.) *Are.*
- Fill in the blanks so that the word spells **are.**

f. (Repeat step *d* for **3. said, 4. shop.**)

g. Get ready to spell the words you just wrote.

h. Look at word 1. What word? (Signal.) *March.*
- Spell **march.** Get ready. (Signal.) *M-A-R-C-H.*
- Fix it if it's not spelled right.

i. (Repeat step *h* for **2. are, 3. said, 4. shop.**)

EXERCISE 2
PATTERNS

a. (Write on the board:)

1. shot	4. got
2. not	5. dog
3. drop	6. lot

- All these words have an **ooo** sound that is spelled with the letter **O.**

- Look at the words and spell them. Then I'll call on individual students to spell them without looking.
b. Word 1: **shot.** Spell **shot.** Get ready. (Signal.) *S-H-O-T.*
c. Word 2: **not.** Spell **not.** Get ready. (Signal.) *N-O-T.*
d. (Repeat step c for **3. drop, 4. got, 5. dog, 6. lot.**)
e. (Erase the board.)
f. (Call on a student.) Spell **shot.** *S-H-O-T.*
g. (Call on another student.) Spell **not.** *N-O-T.*
h. (Repeat step g for **3. drop, 4. got, 5. dog, 6. lot.**)

EXERCISE 3
SENTENCE WRITING

a. Listen to this sentence: **What can we do?**
b. Say that sentence. Get ready. (Signal.) *What can we do?*
c. Write the sentence. ✔
d. I'll spell each word. Check your work. Make an **X** next to any word you got wrong.
e. First word: **What.** W-H-A-T.
f. Next word: **can.** C-A-N.
g. (Repeat step f for **we, do.**)

LESSON 113

EXERCISE 1
SAY THE SOUNDS

a. Listen: **shop.** Say it. (Signal.) *Shop.*
b. What's the first sound in **shop?** (Signal.) *sh.*

> **To Correct**
> - Listen: **sh . . . ooo . . . p.**
> - (Repeat step b.)

c. Next sound? (Signal.) *ooo.*
d. Next sound? (Signal.) *p.*
   Yes. Those are the sounds in **shop.**

e. (Repeat steps a–d for **chin, glad, drop.**)
f. (Call on individual students to say the sounds in **shop, chin, glad, drop.**)

EXERCISE 2
SPELLING WORDS

a. (Write on the board:)

> 1. there
> 2. come
> 3. also
> 4. what

b. Word 1 is **there.**
- Spell **there.** Get ready. (Signal.) *T-H-E-R-E.*
c. Word 2 is **come.**
- Spell **come.** Get ready. (Signal.) *C-O-M-E.*
d. (Repeat step c for **3. also, 4. what.**)
- (Erase the board.)
e. Spell those words without looking.
f. Word 1 is **there.**
- Spell **there.** Get ready. (Signal.) *T-H-E-R-E.*
g. Word 2 is **come.**
- Spell **come.** Get ready. (Signal.) *C-O-M-E.*
h. (Repeat step g for **3. also, 4. what.**)

EXERCISE 3
SENTENCE WRITING

a. Listen to this sentence: **The tall dad is glad.**
b. Say that sentence. Get ready. (Signal.) *The tall dad is glad.*
c. Write the sentence. ✔
d. I'll spell each word. Check your work. Make an **X** next to any word you got wrong.
e. First word: **The.** T-H-E.
f. Next word: **tall.** T-A-L-L.
g. (Repeat step f for **dad, is, glad.**)

LESSON 114

EXERCISE 1
COPYING

a. (Write on the board:)

> **She has many friends.**

- I'll read the sentence on the board: **She has many friends.**
b. Spell **She.** Get ready. (Signal.) *S-H-E.*
- Spell **has.** Get ready. (Signal.) *H-A-S.*
- Spell **many.** Get ready. (Signal.) *M-A-N-Y.*
- Spell **friends.** Get ready. (Signal.) *F-R-I-E-N-D-S.*
c. Copy this sentence on lined paper.
d. (Pause, then check and correct.)
- Read the sentence you just copied. Get ready. (Signal.) *She has many friends.*

EXERCISE 2
PATTERNS

a. You're going to spell words with either the sound **aaa** or **ooo.**
b. Word 1: **shot.** Spell **shot.** Get ready. (Signal.) *S-H-O-T.*
c. Word 2: **mad.** Spell **mad.** Get ready. (Signal.) *M-A-D.*
d. (Repeat step c for **3. sod, 4. hot, 5. fan, 6. got.**)
e. (Erase the board.)
f. You're going to write some of those words.
g. Word 1 is **sod.** What word? (Signal.) *Sod.*
- Write **sod.** ✔
h. Word 2 is **fan.** What word? (Signal.) *Fan.*
- Write **fan.** ✔
i. Word 3 is **mad.** What word? (Signal.) *Mad.*
- Write **mad.** ✔
j. Word 4 is **got.** What word? (Signal.) *Got.*
- Write **got.** ✔
k. Check your work. Make an **X** next to any word you got wrong.
l. Word 1. Spell **sod.** Get ready. (Tap for each letter.) *S-O-D.*
- (Repeat for **2. fan, 3. mad, 4. got.**)

EXERCISE 3
SPELLING REVIEW

a. Get ready to spell and write some words.
b. Word 1 is **what.** What word? (Signal.) *What.*
- Spell **what.** Get ready. (Signal.) *W-H-A-T.*
- Write it. ✔
c. Word 2 is **there.** What word? (Signal.) *There.*

- Spell **there.** Get ready. (Signal.) *T-H-E-R-E.*
- Write it. ✔
d. (Repeat step c for **3. they, 4. farm.**)
e. I'll spell each word.
- Put an **X** next to any word you missed and write that word correctly.
- (Spell each word twice. Write the words on the board as you spell them.)

LESSON 115

EXERCISE 1
SENTENCE REVIEW

a. (Write on the board:)

She has many friends.

- I'll read the sentence on the board: **She has many friends.**
b. Spell **She.** Get ready. (Signal.) *S-H-E.*
- Spell **has.** Get ready. (Signal.) *H-A-S.*
- Spell **many.** Get ready. (Signal.) *M-A-N-Y.*
- Spell **friends.** Get ready. (Signal.) *F-R-I-E-N-D-S.*
c. (Erase the board.)
d. Now let's spell the words in that sentence without looking.
- Spell **She.** Get ready. (Signal.) *S-H-E.*
- Spell **has.** Get ready. (Signal.) *H-A-S.*
- Spell **many.** Get ready. (Signal.) *M-A-N-Y.*
- Spell **friends.** Get ready. (Signal.) *F-R-I-E-N-D-S.*

EXERCISE 2
SAY THE SOUNDS

a. Listen: **lots.** Say it. (Signal.) *Lots.*
b. What's the first sound in **lots?** (Signal.) *lll.*

To Correct
- Listen: **lll . . . ooo . . . t . . . sss.**
- (Repeat step b.)

c. Next sound? (Signal.) *ooo.*
d. Next sound? (Signal.) *t.*
e. Next sound? (Signal.) *sss.*
  Yes. Those are the sounds in **lots.**
f. (Repeat a–e for **math, belt, these.**)

g. (Call on individual students to say the sounds in **lots, math, belt, these.**)

EXERCISE 3
SENTENCE WRITING

a. Listen to this sentence: **They are on the farm.**
b. Say that sentence. Get ready. (Signal.) *They are on the farm.*
c. Write the sentence. ✔
d. I'll spell each word. Check your work. Make an **X** next to any word you got wrong.
e. First word: **They.** T-H-E-Y.
f. Next word: **are.** A-R-E.
g. (Repeat step *f* for **on, the, farm.**)

SENTENCE COMPLETION
EXERCISE 1

a. (Write on the board:)

> Sh_ _ _s _a_y _ _ie_ _ s.

• The sentence should say: **She has many friends.**
b. Write that sentence on lined paper. Fill in the blanks. ✔
c. Now let's spell those words without looking.
• Spell **She.** Get ready. (Signal.) *S-H-E.*
• Spell **has.** Get ready. (Signal.) *H-A-S.*
• Spell **many.** Get ready. (Signal.) *M-A-N-Y.*
• Spell **friends.** Get ready. (Signal.) *F-R-I-E-N-D-S.*
d. (Write to show:)

> She has many friends.

e. Fix up any words you missed. ✔

EXERCISE 2
IDENTIFYING SPELLED WORDS

a. I'll spell some words. See if you can tell which word I spell.
b. Listen to this word: **H-E.** What word? (Signal.) *He.*
c. Listen: **M-E-T.** What word? (Signal.) *Met.*
d. (Repeat step *c* for **mop, at, sit, are.**)
e. (Call on individual students to identify **he, met, mop, at, sit, are** from their spellings.)

EXERCISE 3
SENTENCE WRITING

a. Listen to this sentence: **What did they do?**
b. Say that sentence. Get ready. (Signal.) *What did they do?*
c. Write the sentence. ✔
d. I'll spell each word. Check your work. Make an **X** next to any word you got wrong.
e. First word: **What.** W-H-A-T.
f. Next word: **did.** D-I-D.
g. (Repeat step *f* for **they, do.**)

EXERCISE 1
SENTENCE COMPLETION

a. (Write on the board:)

> _ _ _ _ _s _a_y _ _ie_ _ _.

• The sentence should say: **She has many friends.**
b. Write that sentence on lined paper. Fill in the blanks. ✔
c. Now let's spell those words without looking.
• Spell **She.** Get ready. (Signal.) *S-H-E.*
• Spell **has.** Get ready. (Signal.) *H-A-S.*
• Spell **many.** Get ready. (Signal.) *M-A-N-Y.*
• Spell **friends.** Get ready. (Signal.) *F-R-I-E-N-D-S.*

d. (Write to show:)

> S h e   h a s   many   f r i e n d s.

e. Fix up any words you missed. ✔

EXERCISE 2
SPELLING WORDS

a. (Write on the board:)

> house
> toy
> have

b. Get ready to read these words.
- First word: **house.** What word? (Signal.) *House.*
c. Next word: **toy.** What word? (Signal.) *Toy.*
- (Repeat for **have.**)
d. Now spell those words.
- Spell **house.** Get ready. (Signal.) *H-O-U-S-E.*
e. Spell **toy.** Get ready. (Signal.) *T-O-Y.*
- (Repeat for **have.**)
f. (Erase the board.)
- Spell the words without looking.
g. Spell **house.** Get ready. (Signal.) *H-O-U-S-E.*
h. Spell **toy.** Get ready. (Signal.) *T-O-Y.*
- (Repeat for **have.**)

EXERCISE 3
SPELLING REVIEW

a. Get ready to spell and write some words.
b. Word 1 is **shot.** What word? (Signal.) *Shot.*
- Spell **shot.** Get ready. (Signal.) *S-H-O-T.*
- Write it. ✔
c. Word 2 is **pan.** What word? (Signal.) *Pan.*
- Spell **pan.** Get ready. (Signal.) *P-A-N.*
- Write it. ✔
d. (Repeat step *c* for **3. there, 4. chin.**)
e. I'll spell each word.
- Put an **X** next to any word you missed and write that word correctly.
- (Spell each word twice. Write the words on the board as you spell them.)

LESSON 118

EXERCISE 1
SENTENCE COMPLETION

a. (Write on the board:)

> _ _ _   _ _ _   _a_ _   _ _ie_ _ _.

- The sentence should say: **She has many friends.**
b. Write that sentence on lined paper. Fill in the blanks. ✔
c. Now let's spell those words without looking.
- Spell **She.** Get ready. (Signal.) *S-H-E.*
- Spell **has.** Get ready. (Signal.) *H-A-S.*
- Spell **many.** Get ready. (Signal.) *M-A-N-Y.*
- Spell **friends.** Get ready. (Signal.) *F-R-I-E-N-D-S.*
d. (Write to show:)

> S h e   h a s   many   f r i e n d s.

e. Fix any words you missed. ✔

EXERCISE 2
SPELLING WORDS

a. (Write on the board:)

> 1. toy
> 2. also
> 3. have
> 4. house

b. Word 1 is **toy.** Spell **toy.** Get ready. (Signal.) *T-O-Y.*
c. Word 2 is **also.** Spell **also.** Get ready. (Signal.) *A-L-S-O.*
d. (Repeat step *c* for **3. have, 4. house.**)
- (Erase the board.)
e. Spell those words without looking.
f. Word 1 is **toy.** Spell **toy.** Get ready. (Signal.) *T-O-Y.*
g. Word 2 is **also.** Spell **also.** Get ready. (Signal.) *A-L-S-O.*
h. (Repeat step *g* for **3. have, 4. house.**)

EXERCISE 3
SPELLING REVIEW

a. Get ready to spell and write some words.
b. Word 1 is **inch.** What word? (Signal.) *Inch.*
• Spell **inch.** Get ready. (Signal.) *I-N-C-H.*
• Write it. ✔
c. Word 2 is **back.** What word? (Signal.) *Back.*
• Spell **back.** Get ready. (Signal.) *B-A-C-K.*
• Write it. ✔
d. (Repeat step *c* for **3. come, 4. sand.**)
e. I'll spell each word.
• Put an **X** next to any word you missed and write that word correctly.
• (Spell each word twice. Write the words on the board as you spell them.)

LESSON 119

SENTENCE COMPLETION
EXERCISE 1

a. (Write on the board:)

> _ _ _   _ _ _   _ _ _ _
> _ _i_ _ _ _.

• The sentence should say: **She has many friends.**
b. Write that sentence on lined paper. Fill in the blanks. ✔
c. Now let's spell those words without looking.
• Spell **She.** Get ready. (Signal.) *S-H-E.*
• Spell **has.** Get ready. (Signal.) *H-A-S.*
• Spell **many.** Get ready. (Signal.) *M-A-N-Y.*
• Spell **friends.** Get ready. (Signal.) *F-R-I-E-N-D-S.*
d. (Write to show:)

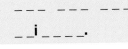
> She has many
> friends.

e. Fix any words you missed. ✔

EXERCISE 2
IDENTIFYING SPELLED WORDS

a. I'll spell some words. See if you can tell which word I spell.
b. Listen to this word: **H-O-T.**
• What word? (Signal.) *Hot.*
c. Listen: **H-O-P.**
• What word? (Signal.) *Hop.*
d. (Repeat step *c* for **he, met, sat.**)
e. (Call on individual students to identify **he, met, sat** from their spellings.)

EXERCISE 3
SENTENCE WRITING

a. Listen to this sentence: **She saw a rat there.**
b. Say that sentence. Get ready. (Signal.) *She saw a rat there.*
c. Write the sentence. ✔
d. I'll spell each word. Check your work. Make an **X** next to any word you got wrong.
e. First word: **She.** S-H-E.
f. Next word: **saw.** S-A-W.
g. (Repeat step *f* for **a, rat, there.**)

LESSON 120

EXERCISE 1
SENTENCE COMPLETION

a. (Write on the board:)

> _ _ _   _ _ _   _ _ _ _   _ _i_ _ _ _.

• The sentence should say: **She has many friends.**
b. Write that sentence on lined paper. Fill in the blanks. ✔
c. Now let's spell those words without looking.
• Spell **She.** Get ready. (Signal.) *S-H-E.*
• Spell **has.** Get ready. (Signal.) *H-A-S.*
• Spell **many.** Get ready. (Signal.) *M-A-N-Y.*
• Spell **friends.** Get ready. (Signal.) *F-R-I-E-N-D-S.*

d. (Write to show:)

> **She has many friends.**

e. Fix any words you missed. ✔

EXERCISE 2
SAY THE SOUNDS

a. Listen: **that.** Say it. (Signal.) *That.*

b. What's the first sound in **that?** (Signal.) *th.*

> **To Correct** ─────
> - Listen: **th . . . aaa . . . t.**
> - (Repeat step *b*.)

c. Next sound? (Signal.) *aaa.*

d. Next sound? (Signal.) *t.*
Yes. Those are the sounds in **that.**

e. (Repeat steps *a–d* for **with, wish, fist.**)

f. (Call on individual students to say the sounds in **that, with, wish, fist.**)

EXERCISE 3
SENTENCE WRITING

a. Listen to this sentence: **They met at a shop.**

b. Say that sentence. Get ready. (Signal.) *They met at a shop.*

c. Write the sentence. ✔

d. I'll spell each word. Check your work. Make an **X** next to any word you got wrong.

e. First word: **They.** T-H-E-Y.

f. Next word: **met.** M-E-T.

g. (Repeat step *f* for **at, a, shop.**)

LESSON 121

EXERCISE 1
SENTENCE WRITING

a. You're going to write this sentence: **She has many friends.**

b. Say the sentence. Get ready. (Signal.) *She has many friends.*

c. Write the sentence. ✔

d. (Write on the board:)

> **She has many friends.**

e. Check your work. Make an **X** next to any word you got wrong.

f. Word 1. Spell **She.** Get ready. (Tap for each letter.) *S-H-E.*

- (Repeat for **has, many, friends.**)

EXERCISE 2
SPELLING WORDS

a. (Write on the board:)

> 1. house
> 2. his
> 3. toy
> 4. barn

b. Word 1 is **house.**

- Spell **house.** Get ready. (Signal.) *H-O-U-S-E.*

c. Word 2 is **his.**

- Spell **his.** Get ready. (Signal.) *H-I-S.*

d. (Repeat step *c* for **3. toy, 4. barn.**)

- (Erase the board.)

e. Spell those words without looking.

f. Word 1 is **house.**

- Spell **house.** Get ready. (Signal.) *H-O-U-S-E.*

g. Word 2 is **his.**

- Spell **his.** Get ready. (Signal.) *H-I-S.*

h. (Repeat step *g* for **3. toy, 4. barn.**)

EXERCISE 3
PROMPTED REVIEW

a. (Write on the board:)

> 1. friends
> 2. house
> 3. many
> 4. have

b. Word 1 is **friends.** Spell **friends.** Get ready. (Signal.) *F-R-I-E-N-D-S.*

c. Word 2 is **house.** Spell **house.** Get ready. (Signal.) *H-O-U-S-E.*

d. (Repeat step *c* for **3. many, 4. have.**)

e. (Erase the board.)
• Now spell those words without looking.
f. Word 1 is **friends**. Spell **friends**. Get ready. (Signal.) *F-R-I-E-N-D-S.*
g. Word 2 is **house**. Spell **house**. Get ready. (Signal.) *H-O-U-S-E.*
h. (Repeat step *g* for **3. many, 4. have.**)
i. (Give individual turns on **1. friends, 2. house, 3. many, 4. have.**)

LESSON 122

EXERCISE 1
IDENTIFYING SPELLED WORDS

a. I'll spell some words. See if you can tell which word I spell.
b. Listen to this word: **H-O-T.**
• What word? (Signal.) *Hot.*
c. Listen: **P-E-T.**
• What word? (Signal.) *Pet.*
d. (Repeat step *c* for **map, shop, sat.**)
e. (Call on individual students to identify **hot, pet, map, shop, sat** from their spellings.)

EXERCISE 2
SPELLING WORDS

a. (Write on the board:)

> 1. have
> 2. fist
> 3. these
> 4. drop

b. Word 1 is **have.**
• Spell **have.** Get ready. (Signal.) *H-A-V-E.*
c. Word 2 is **fist.**
• Spell **fist.** Get ready. (Signal.) *F-I-S-T.*
d. (Repeat step *c* for **3. these, 4. drop.**)
• (Erase the board.)
e. Spell those words without looking.
f. Word 1 is **have.**
• Spell **have.** Get ready. (Signal.) *H-A-V-E.*
g. Word 2 is **fist.**

• Spell **fist.** Get ready. (Signal.) *F-I-S-T.*
h. (Repeat step *g* for **3. these, 4. drop.**)

EXERCISE 3
SPELLING REVIEW

a. Get ready to spell and write some words.
b. Word 1 is **toy.** What word? (Signal.) *Toy.*
• Spell **toy.** Get ready. (Signal.) *T-O-Y.*
• Write it. ✔
c. Word 2 is **there.** What word? (Signal.) *There.*
• Spell **there.** Get ready. (Signal.) *T-H-E-R-E.*
• Write it. ✔
d. (Repeat step *c* for **3. house, 4. belt.**)
e. I'll spell each word. Put an **X** next to any word you missed and write that word correctly.
• (Spell each word twice. Write the words on the board as you spell them.)

LESSON 123

EXERCISE 1
IDENTIFYING SPELLED WORDS

a. I'll spell some words. See if you can tell which word I spell.
b. Listen to this word: **T-H-E.**
• What word? (Signal.) *The.*
c. Listen: **S-H-O-P.**
• What word? (Signal.) *Shop.*
d. (Repeat step *c* for **that, far, hit.**)
e. Your turn to spell those words.
f. **The.** What word? (Signal.) *The.*
• Spell **the.** Get ready. (Signal.) *T-H-E.*
g. **Shop.** What word? (Signal.) *Shop.*
• Spell **shop.** Get ready. (Signal.) *S-H-O-P.*
h. (Repeat step *g* for **that, far, hit.**)

EXERCISE 2
SAY THE SOUNDS

a. Listen: **last.** Say it. (Signal.) *Last.*
b. What's the first sound in **last?** (Signal.) *lll.*

To Correct

- Listen: lll . . . aaa . . . sss . . . t.
- (Repeat step *b*.)

c. Next sound? (Signal.) *aaa.*
d. Next sound? (Signal.) *sss.*
e. Next sound? (Signal.) *t.*
   Yes. Those are the sounds in **last.**
f. (Repeat steps *a–e* for **rats, rest, list.**)
g. (Call on individual students to say the sounds in **last, rats, rest, list.**)

EXERCISE 3
SPELLING REVIEW

a. Get ready to spell and write some words.
b. Word 1 is **shop.** What word? (Signal.) *Shop.*
- Spell **shop.** Get ready. (Signal.) *S-H-O-P.*
- Write it. ✔
c. Word 2 is **these.** What word? (Signal.) *These.*
- Spell **these.** Get ready. (Signal.) *T-H-E-S-E.*
- Write it. ✔
d. (Repeat step *c* for **3. barn, 4. rest.**)
e. I'll spell each word. Put an **X** next to any word you missed and write that word correctly.
- (Spell each word twice. Write the words on the board as you spell them.)

LESSON 124

EXERCISE 1
SAY THE SOUNDS

a. Listen: **those.** Say it. (Signal.) *Those.*
b. What's the first sound in **those?** (Signal.) *th.*

To Correct

- Listen: th . . . ōōō . . . zzz.
- (Repeat step *b*.)

c. Next sound? (Signal.) *ōōō.*

d. Next sound? (Signal.) *zzz.*
   Yes. Those are the sounds in **those.**
e. (Repeat steps *a–d* for **lots, belt, slip.**)
f. (Call on individual students to say the sounds in **those, lots, belt, slip.**)

EXERCISE 2
SPELLING WORDS

a. (Write on the board:)

> some
> every
> does

b. Get ready to read these words. First word: **some.** What word? (Signal.) *Some.*
c. Next word: **every.** What word? (Signal.) *Every.*
- (Repeat for **does.**)
d. Now spell those words. Spell **some.** Get ready. (Signal.) *S-O-M-E.*
e. Spell **every.** Get ready. (Signal.) *E-V-E-R-Y.*
- (Repeat for **does.**)
f. (Erase the board.)
   Spell the words without looking.
g. Spell **some.** Get ready. (Signal.) *S-O-M-E.*
h. Spell **every.** Get ready. (Signal.) *E-V-E-R-Y.*
- (Repeat for **does.**)

EXERCISE 3
SPELLING REVIEW

a. Get ready to spell and write some words.
b. Word 1 is **mad.** What word? (Signal.) *Mad.*
- Spell **mad.** Get ready. (Signal.) *M-A-D.*
- Write it. ✔
c. Word 2 is **get.** What word? (Signal.) *Get.*
- Spell **get.** Get ready. (Signal.) *G-E-T.*
- Write it. ✔
d. (Repeat step *c* for **3. rot, 4. are.**)
e. I'll spell each word. Put an **X** next to any word you missed and write that word correctly.
- (Spell each word twice. Write the words on the board as you spell them.)

LESSON 125

EXERCISE 1
SAY THE SOUNDS

a. Listen: **smooth.** Say it. (Signal.) *Smooth.*

b. What's the first sound in **smooth?** (Signal.) *sss.*

> **To Correct**
> • Listen: **sss . . . mmm . . . oooo . . . th.**
> • (Repeat step *b*.)

c. Next sound? (Signal.) *mmm.*

d. Next sound? (Signal.) *oooo.*

e. Next sound? (Signal.) *th.*
   Yes. Those are the sounds in **smooth.**

f. (Repeat steps *a–e* for **math, dish, ship.**)

g. (Call on individual students to say the sounds in **smooth, math, dish, ship.**)

EXERCISE 2
SPELLING WORDS

a. (Write on the board:)

> 1. does
> 2. rest
> 3. every
> 4. some

b. Word 1 is **does.**
• Spell **does.** Get ready. (Signal.) *D-O-E-S.*

c. Word 2 is **rest.**
• Spell **rest.** Get ready. (Signal.) *R-E-S-T.*

d. (Repeat step *c* for **3. every, 4. some.**)
• (Erase the board.)

e. Spell those words without looking.

f. Word 1 is **does.**
• Spell **does.** Get ready. (Signal.) *D-O-E-S.*

g. Word 2 is **rest.**
• Spell **rest.** Get ready. (Signal.) *R-E-S-T.*

h. (Repeat step *g* for **3. every, 4. some.**)

EXERCISE 3
PROMPTED REVIEW

a. (Write on the board:)

> 1. house
> 2. does
> 3. she
> 4. many

b. Word 1 is **house.**
• Spell **house.** Get ready. (Signal.) *H-O-U-S-E.*

c. Word 2 is **does.**
• Spell **does.** Get ready. (Signal.) *D-O-E-S.*

d. (Repeat step *c* for **3. she, 4. many.**)

e. (Erase the board.)
• Now spell those words without looking.

f. Word 1 is **house.**
• Spell **house.** Get ready. (Signal.) *H-O-U-S-E.*

g. Word 2 is **does.**
• Spell **does.** Get ready. (Signal.) *D-O-E-S.*

h. (Repeat step *g* for **3. she, 4. many.**)

i. (Give individual turns on **1. house, 2. does, 3. she, 4. many.**)

LESSON 126

EXERCISE 1
AFFIXES

a. You're going to write words on lined paper. Number your paper from 1 through 4. ✔

b. Word 1 is **ship.** What word? (Signal.) *Ship.*
• Write the word **ship.** ✔

c. Word 2 is **toy.** What word? (Signal.) *Toy.*
• Write the word **toy.** ✔

d. Word 3 is **belt.** What word? (Signal.) *Belt.*
• Write the word **belt.** ✔

e. Word 4 is **chin.** What word? (Signal.) *Chin.*
• Write the word **chin.** ✔

f. (Write on the board:)

> 1. ship + s =
> 2. toy + s =
> 3. belt + s =
> 4. chin + s =

- Now you're going to add **S** to these words.

g. After **ship** write a plus mark. ✔
After **S** write an equal sign. ✔

h. Write a plus sign, and then **S,** and then an equal sign to the rest of the words. ✔

i. You're going to add **S** to each word to make new words.

j. Word 1 is **ships.** What word? (Signal.) *Ships.*

- Write the word **ships** after the equal sign. ✔

- (Write to show:)

> 1. ship + s = ships

- Here's what you should have: **ship** plus **S** equals **ships.**

k. Word 2 is **toys.** What word? (Signal.) *Toys.*

- Write the word **toys** after the equal sign. ✔

l. Word 3 is **belts.** What word? (Signal.) *Belts.*

- Write the word belts after the equal sign. ✔

m. Word 4 is **chins.** What word? (Signal.) *Chins.*

- Write the word **chins** after the equal sign. ✔

n. Check your work. Make an **X** next to any word you got wrong.

o. Word 1. Spell **ships.** Get ready. (Tap for each letter.) *S-H-I-P-S.*

- (Repeat for **2. toys, 3. belts, 4. chins.**)

EXERCISE 2
PATTERNS

a. Here's a rule about short words that end in the **lll** sound. You spell that sound with two **L**s if you don't hear a letter name.

b. Listen: **fall.** What word? (Signal.) *Fall.*

- Do you hear a letter name in **fall?** (Signal.) *No.*

- So the **lll** sound is spelled with two **L**s: F-A-L-L.

c. New word: **pale.**
What word? (Signal.) *Pale.*

- Do you hear a letter name? (Signal.) *Yes.* Yes, **A** is in **pale.**

- So the **lll** sound is not spelled with two **L**s.

d. New word: **fill.**
What word? (Signal.) *Fill.*

- Do you hear a letter name? (Signal.) *No.*

- So how many **L**s are in **fill?** (Signal.) *Two.* Yes, F-I-L-L.

e. New word: **file.**
What word? (Signal.) *File.*

- Do you hear a letter name? (Signal.) *Yes.* Yes, **I** is in **file.**

- So how many **L**s are in **file?** (Signal.) *One.*

f. New word: **bull.**
What word? (Signal.) *Bull.*

- Do you hear a letter name? (Signal.) *No.*

- So how many **L**s are in **bull?** (Signal.) *Two.*

g. Later, you'll spell words that end with two **L**s.

EXERCISE 3
SENTENCE WRITING

a. Listen to this sentence: **Her friends are there.**

b. Say that sentence. Get ready. (Signal.) *Her friends are there.*

c. Write the sentence. ✔

d. I'll spell each word. Check your work. Make an **X** next to any word you got wrong.

e. First word: **Her.** H-E-R.

f. Next word: **friends.** F-R-I-E-N-D-S.

g. (Repeat step *f* for **are, there.**)

LESSON 127

EXERCISE 1
AFFIXES

a. (Write on the board:)

> 1. mop + s =
> 2. card + s =
> 3. pan + s =
> 4. stop + s =

b. Copy the board. ✔
c. Add **S** to make new words. ✔
d. Check your work. Make an **X** next to any word you got wrong.
e. Word 1. Spell **mops**. Get ready. (Tap for each letter.) *M-O-P-S.*
• (Repeat for **2. cards, 3. pans, 4. stops.**)

EXERCISE 2
PATTERNS

a. You learned a rule about short words that end in the **lll** sound. You spell that sound with two **L**s if the vowel is not the letter name.
b. Listen: **deal**. What word? (Signal.) *Deal.*
• Do you hear a letter name in **deal?** (Signal.) *Yes.*
Yes, **E** is in **deal.**
• So the **lll** sound is spelled with one **L**: **D-E-A-L.**
c. New word: **pill.** What word? (Signal.) *Pill.*
• Do you hear a letter name? (Signal.) *No.*
• So the **lll** sound is spelled with two **L**s. **P-I-L-L.**
d. New word: **small.** What word? (Signal.) *Small.*
• Do you hear a letter name? (Signal.) *No.*
• So how many **L**s are in **small?** (Signal.) *Two.*
e. New word: **ball.** What word? (Signal.) *Ball.*

• Do you hear a letter name? (Signal.) *No.*
• So how many **L**s are in **ball?** (Signal.) *Two.*
f. New word: **chill.** What word? (Signal.) *Chill.*
• Do you hear a letter name? (Signal.) *No.*
• So how many **L**s are in **chill?** (Signal.) *Two.*
g. You're going to write words that have two **L**s. Number your paper from 1 through 4. ✔
h. Word 1 is **ball.** What word? (Signal.) *Ball.*
• Write the word **ball.** ✔
i. Word 2 is **chill.** What word? (Signal.) *Chill.*
• Write the word **chill.** ✔
j. Word 3 is **swell.** What word? (Signal.) *Swell.*
• Write the word **swell.** ✔
k. Word 4 is **doll.** What word? (Signal.) *Doll.*
• Write the word **doll.** ✔
l. Check your work. Make an **X** next to any word you got wrong.
m. Word 1. Spell **ball.** Get ready. (Tap for each letter.) *B-A-L-L.*
• (Repeat for **2. chill, 3. swell, 4. doll.**)

EXERCISE 3
SENTENCE WRITING

a. Listen to this sentence: **That house is his.**
b. Say that sentence. Get ready. (Signal.) *That house is his.*
c. Write the sentence. ✔
d. I'll spell each word. Check your work. Make an **X** next to any word you got wrong.
e. First word: **That.** T-H-A-T.
f. Next word: **house.** H-O-U-S-E.
g. (Repeat step *f* for **is, his.**)

LESSON 128

EXERCISE 1
IDENTIFYING SPELLED WORDS

a. I'll spell some words.
- See if you can tell which word I spell.

b. Listen to this word: **P-A-N-S.**
- What word? (Signal.) *Pans.*

c. Listen: **S-I-T.**
- What word? (Signal.) *Sit.*

d. (Repeat step *c* for **are, it, me.**)

e. Your turn to spell those words.

f. **Pans.** What word? (Signal.) *Pans.*
- Spell **pans.** Get ready. (Signal.) *P-A-N-S.*

g. **Sit.** What word? (Signal.) *Sit.*
- Spell **sit.** Get ready. (Signal.) *S-I-T.*

h. (Repeat step *g* for **are, it, me.**)

EXERCISE 2
SPELLING WORDS

a. (Write on the board:)

> 1. friends
> 2. have
> 3. every
> 4. chill

b. Word 1 is **friends.**
- Spell **friends.** Get ready. (Signal.)
  F-R-I-E-N-D-S.

c. Word 2 is **have.**
- Spell **have.** Get ready. (Signal.) *H-A-V-E.*

d. (Repeat step *c* for **3. every, 4. chill.**)
- (Erase the board.)

e. Spell those words without looking.

f. Word 1 is **friends.**
- Spell **friends.** Get ready. (Signal.)
  F-R-I-E-N-D-S.

g. Word 2 is **have.**
- Spell **have.** Get ready. (Signal.) *H-A-V-E.*

h. (Repeat step *g* for **3. every, 4. chill.**)

SPELLING REVIEW
EXERCISE 3

a. Get ready to spell and write some words.

88

b. Word 1 is **spill.** What word? (Signal.)
  Spill.
- Spell **spill.** Get ready. (Signal.) *S-P-I-L-L.*
- Write it. ✔

c. Word 2 is **mops.** What word? (Signal.)
  Mops.
- Spell **mops.** Get ready. (Signal.) *M-O-P-S.*
- Write it. ✔

d. (Repeat step *c* for **3. have, 4. barn.**)

e. I'll spell each word. Put an **X** next to any
word you missed and write that word
correctly.
- (Spell each word twice. Write the words
on the board as you spell them.)

LESSON 129

EXERCISE 1
SAY THE SOUNDS

a. Listen: **mash.** Say it. (Signal.) *Mash.*

b. What's the first sound in **mash?**
(Signal.) *mmm.*

> **To Correct**
> - Listen: **mmm . . . aaa . . . sh.**
> - (Repeat step *b*.)

c. Next sound? (Signal.) *aaa.*

d. Next sound? (Signal.) *sh.*
Yes. Those are the sounds in **mash.**

e. (Repeat steps *a–d* for **sheep, pit, sun.**)

f. (Call on individual students to say the
sounds in **mash, sheep, pit, sun.**)

EXERCISE 2
SPELLING WORDS

a. (Write on the board:)

> 1. swell
> 2. does
> 3. some
> 4. house

b. Word 1 is **swell.**

- Spell **swell.** Get ready. (Signal.) *S-W-E-L-L.*

c. Word 2 is **does.**
- Spell **does.** Get ready. (Signal.) *D-O-E-S.*

d. (Repeat step c for **3. some, 4. house.**)
- (Erase the board.)

e. Spell those words without looking.

f. Word 1 is **swell.**
- Spell **swell.** Get ready. (Signal.) *S-W-E-L-L.*

g. Word 2 is **does.**
- Spell **does.** Get ready. (Signal.) *D-O-E-S.*

h. (Repeat step g for **3. some, 4. house.**)

EXERCISE 3
SPELLING REVIEW

a. Get ready to spell and write some words.

b. Word 1 is **does.** What word? (Signal.) *Does.*
- Spell **does.** Get ready. (Signal.) *D-O-E-S.*
- Write it. ✔

c. Word 2 is **belts.** What word? (Signal.) *Belts.*
- Spell **belts.** Get ready. (Signal.) *B-E-L-T-S.*
- Write it. ✔

d. (Repeat step c for **3. sits, 4. fills.**)

e. I'll spell each word. Put an **X** next to any word you missed and write that word correctly.
- (Spell each word twice. Write the words on the board as you spell them.)

LESSON 130

EXERCISE 1
WORD COMPLETION

a. (Write on the board:)

| 1. ever_ |
| 2. fr _ _nds |
| 3. d _ _s |
| 4. sma_ _ |

b. Copy the board. ✔

c. One or more letters are missing from these words. You're going to write the missing letters.

d. Word 1 is supposed to be **every.**
- What word? (Signal.) *Every.*
- Fill in the blanks so that the word spells **every.**

e. Word 2 is supposed to be **friends.**
- What word? (Signal.) *Friends.*
- Fill in the blanks so that the word spells **friends.**

f. (Repeat step d for **3. does, 4. small.**)

g. Get ready to spell the words you just wrote.

h. Look at word 1.
- What word? (Signal.) *Every.*
- Spell **every.** Get ready. (Signal.) *E-V-E-R-Y.*
- Fix it if it's not spelled right.

i. (Repeat step h for **2. friends, 3. does, 4. small.**)

EXERCISE 2
SPELLING WORDS

a. (Write on the board:)

| 1. bull |
| 2. ships |
| 3. what |
| 4. last |

b. Word 1 is **bull.**
- Spell **bull.** Get ready. (Signal.) *B-U-L-L.*

c. Word 2 is **ships.**
- Spell **ships.** Get ready. (Signal.) *S-H-I-P-S.*

d. (Repeat step c for **3. what, 4. last.**)
- (Erase the board.)

e. Spell those words without looking.

f. Word 1 is **bull.**
- Spell **bull.** Get ready. (Signal.) *B-U-L-L.*

g. Word 2 is **ships.**
- Spell **ships.** Get ready. (Signal.) *S-H-I-P-S.*

h. (Repeat step g for **3. what, 4. last.**)

EXERCISE 3
SENTENCE WRITING

a. Listen to this sentence: **Every pan is hot.**

b. Say that sentence. Get ready. (Signal.) *Every pan is hot.*

c. Write the sentence. ✔

d. I'll spell each word. Check your work. Make an **X** next to any word you got wrong.

e. First word: **Every.** E-V-E-R-Y.

f. Next word: **pan.** P-A-N.

g. (Repeat step *f* for **is, hot.**)

LESSON 131

EXERCISE 1
SENTENCE COPYING

a. (Write on the board:)

> **They read part of the book.**

- I'll read the sentence on the board: **They read part of the book.**

b. Spell **They.** Get ready. (Signal.) *T-H-E-Y.*

- Spell **read.** Get ready. (Signal.) *R-E-A-D.*
- Spell **part.** Get ready. (Signal.) *P-A-R-T.*
- Spell **of.** Get ready. (Signal.) *O-F.*
- Spell **the.** Get ready. (Signal.) *T-H-E.*
- Spell **book.** Get ready. (Signal.) *B-O-O-K.*

c. Copy this sentence on lined paper.

d. (Pause, then check and correct.)

- Read the sentence you just copied. Get ready. (Signal.) *They read part of the book.*

EXERCISE 2
PATTERNS

a. (Write on the board:)

> 1. ring
> 2. thing
> 3. sing
> 4. king

- In each of these words, the sound **ing** is spelled with the letters **I-N-G.**
- Tell me how to spell **ing.** Get ready. (Signal.) *I-N-G.*

b. Word 1 is **ring.** Spell **ring.** Get ready. (Signal.) *R-I-N-G.*

c. Word 2 is **thing.** Spell **thing.** Get ready. (Signal.) *T-H-I-N-G.*

d. (Repeat step *c* for **3. sing, 4. king.**)

- (Erase the board.)

e. Word 1 is **ring.** Spell **ring.** Get ready. (Signal.) *R-I-N-G.*

f. Word 2 is **thing.** Spell **thing.** Get ready. (Signal.) *T-H-I-N-G.*

g. (Repeat step *f* for **3. sing, 4. king.**)

EXERCISE 3
SENTENCE WRITING

a. Listen to this sentence: **The friends have pets.**

b. Say that sentence. Get ready. (Signal.) *The friends have pets.*

c. Write the sentence. ✔

d. I'll spell each word. Check your work. Make an **X** next to any word you got wrong.

e. First word: **The.** T-H-E.

f. Next word: **friends.** F-R-I-E-N-D-S.

g. (Repeat step *f* for **have, pets.**)

LESSON 132

SENTENCE
EXERCISE 1

a. (Write on the board:)

> **They read part of the book.**

- I'll read the sentence on the board: **They read part of the book.**

b. Spell **They.** Get ready. (Signal.) *T-H-E-Y.*

- Spell **read.** Get ready. (Signal.) *R-E-A-D.*
- Spell **part.** Get ready. (Signal.) *P-A-R-T.*
- Spell **of.** Get ready. (Signal.) *O-F.*
- Spell **the.** Get ready. (Signal.) *T-H-E.*
- Spell **book.** Get ready. (Signal.) *B-O-O-K.*

c. (Erase the board.)

d. Now let's spell the words in that sentence without looking.

- Spell **They.** Get ready. (Signal.) *T-H-E-Y.*
- Spell **read.** Get ready. (Signal.) *R-E-A-D.*
- Spell **part.** Get ready. (Signal.) *P-A-R-T.*

- Spell **of.** Get ready. (Signal.) *O-F.*
- Spell **the.** Get ready. (Signal.) *T-H-E.*
- Spell **book.** Get ready. (Signal.) *B-O-O-K.*

EXERCISE 2
PATTERNS

a. (Write on the board:)

> 1. sing
> 2. king
> 3. ring
> 4. thing

- In each of these words, the sound **ing** is spelled with the letters **I-N-G.**
- Tell me how to spell **ing.** Get ready. (Signal.) *I-N-G.*

b. Word 1 is **sing.**
- Spell **sing.** Get ready. (Signal.) *S-I-N-G.*

c. Word 2 is **king.**
- Spell **king.** Get ready. (Signal.) *K-I-N-G.*

d. (Repeat step c for **3. ring, 4. thing.**)
- (Erase the board.)

e. Word 1 is **sing.**
- Spell **sing.** Get ready. (Signal.) *S-I-N-G.*

f. Word 2 is **king.**
- Spell **king.** Get ready. (Signal.) *K-I-N-G.*

g. (Repeat step f for **3. ring, 4. thing.**)

EXERCISE 3
SPELLING REVIEW

a. Get ready to spell and write some words.

b. Word 1 is **swell.** What word? (Signal.) *Swell.*
- Spell **swell.** Get ready. (Signal.) *S-W-E-L-L.*
- Write it. ✔

c. Word 2 is **every.** What word? (Signal.) *Every.*
- Spell **every.** Get ready. (Signal.) *E-V-E-R-Y.*
- Write it. ✔

d. (Repeat step c for **3. have, 4. said.**)

e. I'll spell each word. Put an **X** next to any word you missed and write that word correctly.
- (Spell each word twice. Write the words on the board as you spell them.)

SENTENCE COMPLETION
EXERCISE 1

a. (Write on the board:)

> _ _ey _ea_ _ar_ of _ _e _ook.

- The sentence should say: **They read part of the book.**

b. Write that sentence on lined paper. Fill in the blanks. ✔

c. Now let's spell those words without looking.
- Spell **They.** Get ready. (Signal.) *T-H-E-Y.*
- Spell **read.** Get ready. (Signal.) *R-E-A-D.*
- Spell **part.** Get ready. (Signal.) *P-A-R-T.*
- Spell **of.** Get ready. (Signal.) *O-F.*
- Spell **the.** Get ready. (Signal.) *T-H-E.*
- Spell **book.** Get ready. (Signal.) *B-O-O-K.*

d. (Write to show:)

> T hey read part of t he book.

e. Fix any words you missed. ✔

EXERCISE 2
SPELLING WORDS

a. (Write on the board:)

> 1. thing
> 2. stops
> 3. hill
> 4. does

b. Word 1 is **thing.**
- Spell **thing.** Get ready. (Signal.) *T-H-I-N-G.*

c. Word 2 is **stops.**
- Spell **stops.** Get ready. (Signal.) *S-T-O-P-S.*

d. (Repeat step c for **3. hill, 4. does.**)
- (Erase the board.)

e. Spell those words without looking.

f. Word 1 is **thing.**
- Spell **thing.** Get ready. (Signal.) *T-H-I-N-G.*

g. Word 2 is **stops.**
- Spell **stops.** Get ready. (Signal.) *S-T-O-P-S.*
h. (Repeat step *g* for **3. hill, 4. does.**)

EXERCISE 3
SPELLING REVIEW

a. Get ready to spell and write some words.
b. Word 1 is **shots.** What word? (Signal.) *Shots.*
- Spell **shots.** Get ready. (Signal.) *S-H-O-T-S.*
- Write it. ✔
c. Word 2 is **are.** What word? (Signal.) *Are.*
- Spell **are.** Get ready. (Signal.) *A-R-E.*
- Write it. ✔
d. (Repeat step *c* for **3. ring, 4. glad.**)
e. I'll spell each word. Put an **X** next to any word you missed and write that word correctly.
- (Spell each word twice. Write the words on the board as you spell them.)

LESSON 134

EXERCISE 1
SENTENCE COMPLETION

a. (Write on the board:)

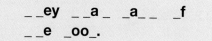

- The sentence should say: **They read part of the book.**
b. Write that sentence on lined paper. Fill in the blanks. ✔
c. Now let's spell those words without looking.
- Spell **They.** Get ready. (Signal.) *T-H-E-Y.*
- Spell **read.** Get ready. (Signal.) *R-E-A-D.*
- Spell **part.** Get ready. (Signal.) *P-A-R-T.*
- Spell **of.** Get ready. (Signal.) *O-F.*
- Spell **the.** Get ready. (Signal.) *T-H-E.*
- Spell **book.** Get ready. (Signal.) *B-O-O-K.*

d. (Write to show:)

> They read part of
> the book.

e. Fix any words you missed. ✔

EXERCISE 2
SPELLING WORDS

a. (Write on the board:)

> 1. house
> 2. tell
> 3. some
> 4. cards

b. Word 1 is **house.**
- Spell **house.** Get ready. (Signal.) *H-O-U-S-E.*
c. Word 2 is **tell.**
- Spell **tell.** Get ready. (Signal.) *T-E-L-L.*
d. (Repeat step *c* for **3. some, 4. cards.**)
- (Erase the board.)
e. Spell those words without looking.
f. Word 1 is **house.**
- Spell **house.** Get ready. (Signal.) *H-O-U-S-E.*
g. Word 2 is **tell.**
- Spell **tell.** Get ready. (Signal.) *T-E-L-L.*
h. (Repeat step *g* for **3. some, 4. cards.**)

EXERCISE 3
PROMPTED REVIEW

a. (Write on the board:)

> 1. thing
> 2. fists
> 3. there
> 4. shop

b. Word 1 is **thing.** Spell **thing.** Get ready. (Signal.) *T-H-I-N-G.*
c. Word 2 is **fists.** Spell **fists.** Get ready. (Signal.) *F-I-S-T-S.*
d. (Repeat step *c* for **3. there, 4. shop.**)
e. (Erase the board.)
- Now spell those words without looking.

f. Word 1 is **thing.** Spell **thing.** Get ready. (Signal.) *T-H-I-N-G.*

g. Word 2 is **fists.** Spell **fists.** Get ready. (Signal.) *F-I-S-T-S.*

h. (Repeat step g for **3. there, 4. shop.**)

i. (Give individual turns on **1. thing, 2. fists, 3. there, 4. shop.**)

LESSON **135**

EXERCISE 1
SENTENCE COMPLETION

a. (Write on the board:)

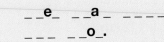
$$\_\_e\_\ \_\_a\_\ \_\_\_\_\ \_\_$$
$$\_\_\_\ \_\_o\_.$$

• The sentence should say: **They read part of the book.**

b. Write that sentence on lined paper. Fill in the blanks. ✔

c. Now let's spell those words without looking.

• Spell **They.** Get ready. (Signal.) *T-H-E-Y.*
• Spell **read.** Get ready. (Signal.) *R-E-A-D.*
• Spell **part.** Get ready. (Signal.) *P-A-R-T.*
• Spell **of.** Get ready. (Signal.) *O-F.*
• Spell **the.** Get ready. (Signal.) *T-H-E.*
• Spell **book.** Get ready. (Signal.) *B-O-O-K.*

d. (Write to show:)

> They read part of
> the book.

e. Fix any words you missed. ✔

EXERCISE 2
SAY THE SOUNDS

a. Listen: **wish.** Say it. (Signal.) *Wish.*

b. What's the first sound in **wish?** (Signal.) *www.*

To Correct
• Listen: **www . . . iii . . . sh.**
• (Repeat step *b.*)

c. Next sound? (Signal.) *iii.*

d. Next sound? (Signal.) *sh.*
Yes. Those are the sounds in **wish.**

e. (Repeat steps a–d for **path, chip, it.**)

f. (Call on individual students to say the sounds in **wish, path, chip, it.**)

EXERCISE 3
SENTENCE WRITING

a. Listen to this sentence: **They get many things.**

b. Say that sentence. Get ready. (Signal.) *They get many things.*

c. Write the sentence. ✔

d. I'll spell each word. Check your work. Make an **X** next to any word you got wrong.

e. First word: **They.** T-H-E-Y.

f. Next word: **get.** G-E-T.

g. (Repeat step *f* for **many, things.**)

LESSON **136**

EXERCISE 1
SENTENCE COMPLETION

a. (Write on the board:)

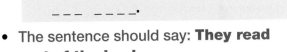
$$\_\_\_\_\ \_\_\_\_\ \_\_\_\_\ \_\_$$
$$\_\_\_\ \_\_\_\_.$$

• The sentence should say: **They read part of the book.**

b. Write that sentence on lined paper. Fill in the blanks. ✔

c. Now let's spell those words without looking.

• Spell **They.** Get ready. (Signal.) *T-H-E-Y.*
• Spell **read.** Get ready. (Signal.) *R-E-A-D.*
• Spell **part.** Get ready. (Signal.) *P-A-R-T.*
• Spell **of.** Get ready. (Signal.) *O-F.*
• Spell **the.** Get ready. (Signal.) *T-H-E.*
• Spell **book.** Get ready. (Signal.) *B-O-O-K.*

d. (Write to show:)

> They read part of
> the book.

e. Fix any words you missed. ✔

EXERCISE 2
IDENTIFYING SPELLED WORDS

a. I'll spell some words. See if you can tell which word I spell.

b. Listen to this word: **S-I-T-S.**
- What word? (Signal.) *Sits.*

c. Listen: **D-I-S-H.**
- What word? (Signal.) *Dish.*

d. (Repeat step c for **fun, slip.**)

e. Your turn to spell those words.

f. **Sits.** What word? (Signal.) *Sits.*
- Spell **sits.** Get ready. (Signal.) *S-I-T-S.*

g. **Dish.** What word? (Signal.) *Dish.*
- Spell **dish.** Get ready. (Signal.) *D-I-S-H.*

h. (Repeat step g for **fun, slip.**)

EXERCISE 3
SPELLING REVIEW

a. Get ready to spell and write some words.

b. Word 1 is **shops.** What word? (Signal.) *Shops.*
- Spell **shops.** Get ready. (Signal.) *S-H-O-P-S.*
- Write it. ✔

c. Word 2 is **rich.** What word? (Signal.) *Rich.*
- Spell **rich.** Get ready. (Signal.) *R-I-C-H.*
- Write it. ✔

d. (Repeat step c for **3. was, 4. on.**)

e. I'll spell each word. Put an **X** next to any word you missed and write that word correctly.
- (Spell each word twice. Write the words on the board as you spell them.)

LESSON 137

EXERCISE 1
SENTENCE WRITING

a. You're going to write this sentence:
They read part of the book.

b. Say the sentence. Get ready. (Signal.) *They read part of the book.*

c. Write the sentence. ✔

d. (Write on the board:)

> **They read part of the book.**

e. Check your work. Make an **X** next to any word you got wrong.

f. Word 1. Spell **They.** Get ready. (Tap for each letter.) *T-H-E-Y.*
- (Repeat for **read, part, of, the, book.**)

EXERCISE 2
AFFIXES

a. You're going to write words on lined paper. Number your paper from 1 through 4. ✔

b. Word 1 is **farm.** What word? (Signal.) *Farm.*
- Write the word **farm.** ✔

c. Word 2 is **wish.** What word? (Signal.) *Wish.*
- Write the word **wish.** ✔

d. Word 3 is **ring.** What word? (Signal.) *Ring.*
- Write the word **ring.** ✔

e. Word 4 is **do.** What word? (Signal.) *Do.*
- Write the word **do.** ✔

f. (Write on the board:)

> 1. farm + ing =
> 2. wish + ing =
> 3. ring + ing =
> 4. do + ing =

- Now you're going to add **ing** to these words.

g. After **farm** write a plus mark and **ing.** ✔ After **ing** write an equal sign. ✔

h. Write a plus sign, and then **ing,** and then an equal sign to the rest of the words. ✔

i. You're going to add **ing** to each word to make new words.

j. Word 1 is **farming.** What word? (Signal.) *Farming.*
- Write the word **farming** after the equal sign. ✔

- (Write to show:)

> farm + ing = farming

- Here's what you should have: **farm** plus **ing** equals **farming**.
k. Word 2 is **wishing.** What word? (Signal.) *Wishing.*
- Write the word **wishing** after the equal sign. ✔
l. Word 3 is **ringing.** What word? (Signal.) *Ringing.*
- Write the word **ringing** after the equal sign. ✔
m. Word 4 is **doing.** What word? (Signal.) *Doing.*
- Write the word **doing** after the equal sign. ✔
n. Check your work. Make an **X** next to any word you got wrong.
o. Word 1. Spell **farming.** Get ready. (Tap for each letter.) *F-A-R-M-I-N-G.*
- (Repeat for **2. wishing, 3. ringing, 4. doing.**)

EXERCISE 3
SENTENCE WRITING

a. Listen to this sentence: **What will they do?**
b. Say that sentence. Get ready. (Signal.) *What will they do?*
c. Write the sentence. ✔
d. I'll spell each word. Check your work. Make an **X** next to any word you got wrong.
e. First word: **What.** W-H-A-T.
f. Next word: **will.** W-I-L-L.
g. (Repeat step *f* for **they, do.**)

LESSON 138

EXERCISE 1
SAY THE SOUNDS

a. Listen: **step.** Say it. (Signal.) *Step.*

b. What's the first sound in **step?** (Signal.) *sss.*

To Correct
- Listen: **sss . . . t . . . eee . . . p.**
- (Repeat step *b.*)

c. Next sound? (Signal.) *t.*
d. Next sound? (Signal.) *eee.*
e. Next sound? (Signal.) *p.*
Yes. Those are the sounds in **step.**
f. (Repeat steps *a–e* for **end, rest, sand.**)
g. (Call on individual students to say the sounds in **step, end, rest, sand.**)

EXERCISE 2
AFFIXES

a. (Write on the board:)

> 1. fish + ing =
> 2. sing + ing =
> 3. tell + ing =
> 4. rock + ing =

b. Copy the board. ✔
c. Add **ing** to make new words. ✔
d. Check your work. Make an **X** next to any word you got wrong.
e. Word 1. Spell **fishing.** Get ready. (Tap for each letter.) *F-I-S-H-I-N-G.*
- (Repeat for **2. singing, 3. telling, 4. rocking.**)

EXERCISE 3
PROMPTED REVIEW

a. (Write on the board:)

> 1. book
> 2. calling
> 3. rings
> 4. frogs

b. Word 1 is **book.** Spell **book.** Get ready. (Signal.) *B-O-O-K.*
c. Word 2 is **calling.** Spell **calling.** Get ready. (Signal.) *C-A-L-L-I-N-G.*
d. (Repeat step *c* for **3. rings, 4. frogs.**)

e. (Erase the board.)
- Now spell those words without looking.
f. Word 1 is **book.** Spell **book.** Get ready. (Signal.) *B-O-O-K.*
g. Word 2 is **calling.** Spell **calling.** Get ready. (Signal.) *C-A-L-L-I-N-G.*
h. (Repeat step *g* for **3. rings, 4. frogs.**)
i. (Give individual turns on **1. book, 2. calling, 3. rings, 4. frogs.**)

LESSON 139

EXERCISE 1
SPELLING WORDS

a. (Write on the board:)

> 1. book
> 2. does
> 3. house
> 4. toy

b. Word 1 is **book.**
- Spell **book.** Get ready. (Signal.) *B-O-O-K.*
c. Word 2 is **does.**
- Spell **does.** Get ready. (Signal.) *D-O-E-S.*
d. (Repeat step *c* for **3. house, 4. toy.**)
- (Erase the board.)
e. Spell those words without looking.
f. Word 1 is **book.**
- Spell **book.** Get ready. (Signal.) *B-O-O-K.*
g. Word 2 is **does.**
- Spell **does.** Get ready. (Signal.) *D-O-E-S.*
h. (Repeat step *g* for **3. house, 4. toy.**)

EXERCISE 2
AFFIXES

a. (Write on the board:)

> 1. pick + ing =
> 2. salt + ing =
> 3. sand + ing =
> 4. fall + ing =

b. Copy the board. ✔
c. Add **ing** to make new words. ✔

d. Check your work. Make an **X** next to any word you got wrong.
e. Word 1. Spell **picking.** Get ready. (Tap for each letter.) *P-I-C-K-I-N-G.*
- (Repeat for **2. salting, 3. sanding, 4. falling.**)

EXERCISE 3
SENTENCE WRITING

a. Listen to this sentence: **We read all of the book.**
b. Say that sentence. Get ready. (Signal.) *We read all of the book.*
c. Write the sentence. ✔
d. I'll spell each word. Check your work. Make an **X** next to any word you got wrong.
e. First word: **We.** W-E.
f. Next word: **read.** R-E-A-D.
g. (Repeat step *f* for **all, of, the, book.**)

LESSON 140

EXERCISE 1
WORD COMPLETION

a. (Write on the board:)

> 1. h_ _se
> 2. _ _at
> 3. th _ _ _

b. Copy the board. ✔
c. One or more letters are missing from these words. You're going to write the missing letters.
d. Word 1 is supposed to be **house.** What word? (Signal.) *House.*
- Fill in the blanks so that the word spells **house.**
e. Word 2 is supposed to be **what.**
- What word? (Signal.) *What.*
- Fill in the blanks so that the word spells **what.**
f. (Repeat step *d* for **3. thing.**)

96

g. Get ready to spell the words you just wrote.

h. Look at word 1.
- What word? (Signal.) *House.*
- Spell **house.** Get ready. (Signal.) *H-O-U-S-E.*
- Fix it if it's not spelled right.

i. (Repeat step *h* for **2. what, 3. thing.**)

EXERCISE 2
IDENTIFYING SPELLED WORDS

a. I'll spell some words. See if you can tell which word I spell.

b. Listen to this word: **H-A-N-D.**
- What word? (Signal.) *Hand.*

c. Listen: **F-I-S-T.**
- What word? (Signal.) *Fist.*

d. (Repeat step *c* for **stand, stall.**)

e. Your turn to spell those words.

f. **Hand.** What word? (Signal.) *Hand.*
- Spell **hand.** Get ready. (Signal.) *H-A-N-D.*

g. **Fist.** What word? (Signal.) *Fist.*
- Spell **fist.** Get ready. (Signal.) *F-I-S-T.*

h. (Repeat step *g* for **stand, stall.**)

EXERCISE 3
SENTENCE WRITING

a. Listen to this sentence: **Where did they stop?**

b. Say that sentence. Get ready. (Signal.) *Where did they stop?*

c. Write the sentence. ✔

d. I'll spell each word. Check your work. Make an **X** next to any word you got wrong.

e. First word: **Where.** W-H-E-R-E.

f. Next word: **did.** D-I-D.

g. (Repeat step *f* for **they, stop.**)

LESSON 141

EXERCISE 1
PATTERN VE

a. The **vvv** sound at the end of words is usually spelled with the letters **V-E.**

b. The sound at the end of **have** is **vvv.** Tell me how to spell that sound. Get ready. (Signal.) *V-E.*
- Spell **have.** Get ready. (Signal.) *H-A-V-E.*

c. What sound is at the end of **gave?** (Signal.) *vvv.*
- Tell me how to spell that sound. Get ready. (Signal.) *V-E.*
- Spell **gave.** Get ready. (Signal.) *G-A-V-E.*

d. (Repeat step *c* for **grave.**)

e. Lets see if you can spell some other words with the sound **vvv.**

f. (Call on a student.) Spell **save.** *S-A-V-E.*

g. (Repeat step *f* for **hive, eve, give, lĭve.**)

EXERCISE 2
SPELLING WORDS

a. (Write on the board:)

> 1. ringing
> 2. paths
> 3. does
> 4. book

b. Word 1 is **ringing.**
- Spell **ringing.** Get ready. (Signal.) *R-I-N-G-I-N-G.*

c. Word 2 is **paths.**
- Spell **paths.** Get ready. (Signal.) *P-A-T-H-S.*

d. (Repeat step *c* for **3. does, 4. book.**)
- (Erase the board.)

e. Spell those words without looking.

f. Word 1 is **ringing.**
- Spell **ringing.** Get ready. (Signal.) *R-I-N-G-I-N-G.*

g. Word 2 is **paths.** Spell **paths.** Get ready. (Signal.) *P-A-T-H-S.*

h. (Repeat step *g* for **3. does, 4. book.**)

EXERCISE 3
SENTENCE WRITING

a. Listen to this sentence: **They read all of the book.**

b. Say that sentence. Get ready. (Signal.) *They read all of the book.*

c. Write the sentence. ✔

d. I'll spell each word. Check your work. Make an **X** next to any word you got wrong.

e. First word: **They.** T-H-E-Y.

f. Next word: **read.** R-E-A-D.

g. (Repeat step *f* for **all, of, the, book.**)

LESSON 142

EXERCISE 1
PATTERN VE

a. What sound is at the end of **save?** (Signal.) *vvv.*

• Tell me how to spell that sound. Get ready. (Signal.) *V-E.*

• Spell **gave.** Get ready. (Signal.) *G-A-V-E.*

b. (Repeat step *a* for **lĭve, five.**)

c. Get ready to spell some other words that end in the sound **vvv.**

d Word 1 is **save.**

• What word? (Signal.) *Save.*

• Spell **save.** Get ready. (Signal.) *S-A-V-E.*

e. (Repeat step *d* for **lĭve, shave, grave.**)

EXERCISE 2
SPELLING WORDS

a. (Write on the board:)

> 1. other
> 2. said
> 3. small
> 4. every
> 5. drops

b. Word 1 is **other.**

• Spell **other.** Get ready. (Signal.) *O-T-H-E-R.*

c. Word 2 is **said.**

• Spell **said.** Get ready. (Signal.) *S-A-I-D.*

d. (Repeat step *c* for **3. small, 4. every, 5. drops.**)

• (Erase the board.)

e. Spell those words without looking.

f. Word 1 is **other.**

• Spell **other.** Get ready. (Signal.) *O-T-H-E-R.*

g. Word 2 is **said.**

• Spell **said.** Get ready. (Signal.) *S-A-I-D.*

h. (Repeat step *g* for **3. small, 4. every, 5. drops.**)

EXERCISE 3
SENTENCE WRITING

a. Listen to this sentence: **They saw many friends.**

b. Say that sentence. Get ready. (Signal.) *They saw many friends.*

c. Write the sentence. ✔

d. I'll spell each word. Check your work. Make an **X** next to any word you got wrong.

e. First word: **They.** T-H-E-Y.

f. Next word: **saw.** S-A-W.

g. (Repeat step *f* for **many, friends.**)

LESSON 143

EXERCISE 1
PATTERN VE

a. What sound is at the end of **wave?** (Signal.) *vvv.*

• Tell me how to spell that sound. Get ready. (Signal.) *V-E.*

• Spell **wave.** Get ready. (Signal.) *W-A-V-E.*

b. (Repeat step *a* for **lĭve, eve, hive.**)

c. Get ready to spell some other words that end in the sound **vvv.**

d. Word 1 is **slave.**

• What word? (Signal.) *Slave.*

• Spell **slave.** Get ready. (Signal.) *S-L-A-V-E.*

e. (Repeat step *d* for **wave, hive, give.**)

EXERCISE 2
SAY THE SOUNDS

a. Listen: **dust.** Say it. (Signal.) *Dust.*

b. Say the sounds in **dust.** Get ready. (Tap for each sound.) *d . . .uuu . . . sss . . . t.*

c. What's the first sound in **dust**? (Signal.) *d.*

d. Next sound? (Signal.) *uuu.*

e. Next sound? (Signal.) *sss.*

f. Next sound? (Signal.) *t.*
Yes. Those are the sounds in **dust.**

g. (Repeat steps *a–f* for **grave, stand, flat.**)

h. (Call on individual students to say the sounds in **dust, grave, stand, flat.**)

EXERCISE 3
SPELLING REVIEW

a. Get ready to spell and write some words.

b. Word 1 is **fill.** What word? (Signal.) *Fill.*

• Spell **fill.** Get ready. (Signal.) *F-I-L-L.*

• Write it. ✔

c. Word 2 is **said.** What word? (Signal.) *Said.*

• Spell **said.** Get ready. (Signal.) *S-A-I-D.*

• Write it. ✔

d. (Repeat step *c* for **3. his, 4. lasting.**)

e. I'll spell each word. Put an **X** next to any word you missed and write that word correctly.

• (Spell each word twice. Write the words on the board as you spell them.)

LESSON 144

EXERCISE 1
SPELLING WORDS

a. (Write on the board:)

> love
> move
> drove
> shove
> glove

b. Get ready to read these words. First word: **love.** What word? (Signal.) *Love.*

c. Next word: **move.** What word? (Signal.) *Move.*

• (Repeat for **drove, shove, glove.**)

d. Now spell those words.

• Spell **love.** Get ready. (Signal.) *L-O-V-E.*

e. Spell **move.** Get ready. (Signal.) *M-O-V-E.*

• (Repeat for **drove, shove, glove.**)

• (Erase the board.)

f. Spell the words without looking.

g. Spell **love.** Get ready. (Signal.) *L-O-V-E.*

h. Spell **move.** Get ready. (Signal.) *M-O-V-E.*

• (Repeat for **drove, shove, glove.**)

EXERCISE 2
IDENTIFYING SPELLED WORDS

a. I'll spell some words. See if you can tell which word I spell.

b. Listen to this word: **L-A-S-T.**

• What word? (Signal.) *Last.*

c. Listen: **I-S.**

• What word? (Signal.) *Is.*

d. (Repeat step *c* for **pick, chin, ball.**)

e. Your turn to spell those words.

f. **Last.** What word? (Signal.) *Last.*

• Spell **last.** Get ready. (Signal.) *L-A-S-T.*

g. **Is.** What word? (Signal.) *Is.*

• Spell **is.** Get ready. (Signal.) *I-S.*

h. (Repeat step *g* for **pick, chin, ball.**)

EXERCISE 3
SENTENCE WRITING

a. Listen to this sentence: **He drops every ball.**

b. Say that sentence. Get ready. (Signal.) *He drops every ball.*

c. Write the sentence. ✔

d. I'll spell each word. Check your work. Make an **X** next to any word you got wrong.

e. First word: **He.** H-E.

f. Next word: **drops.** D-R-O-P-S.

g. (Repeat step *f* for **every, ball.**)

99

LESSON 145

EXERCISE 1
PATTERNS

a. (Write on the board:)

> 1. call
> 2. can
> 3. car
> 4. cat
> 5. cut

- All these words begin with the sound **k** spelled with the letter **C**. Look at the words, and we'll spell them together.

b. Word 1 is **call**.

- Spell **call**. Get ready. (Signal.) *C-A-L-L.*

c. Word 2 is **can**. Spell **can**. Get ready. (Signal.) *C-A-N.*

d. (Repeat step c for **car, cat, cut.**)

e. When I call on you, see if you can spell the word without looking.

f. (Call on a student.) Spell **can**. *C-A-N.*

g. (Call on another student.) Spell **call**. *C-A-L-L.*

h. (Repeat step g for **cut, car, cat.**)

EXERCISE 2
SPELLING WORDS

a. (Write on the board:)

> 1. drove
> 2. move
> 3. shove
> 4. love
> 5. glove

b. Word 1 is **drove**.

- Spell **drove**. Get ready. (Signal.) *D-R-O-V-E.*

c. Word 2 is **move**.

- Spell **move**. Get ready. (Signal.) *M-O-V-E.*

d. (Repeat step c for **3. shove, 4. love, 5. glove.**)

- (Erase the board.)

e. Spell those words without looking.

f. Word 1 is **drove**.

- Spell **drove**. Get ready. (Signal.) *D-R-O-V-E.*

g. Word 2 is **move**.

- Spell **move**. Get ready. (Signal.) *M-O-V-E.*

h. (Repeat step g for **3. shove, 4. love, 5. glove.**)

EXERCISE 3
SPELLING REVIEW

a. Get ready to spell and write some words.

b. Word 1 is **book**. What word? (Signal.) *Book.*

- Spell **book**. Get ready. (Signal.) *B-O-O-K.*
- Write it. ✔

c. Word 2 is **hive**. What word? (Signal.) *Hive.*

- Spell **hive**. Get ready. (Signal.) *H-I-V-E.*
- Write it. ✔

d. (Repeat step c for **3. small, 4. part.**)

e. I'll spell each word. Put an **X** next to any word you missed and write that word correctly.

- (Spell each word twice. Write the words on the board as you spell them.)

LESSON 146

EXERCISE 1
PATTERNS

a. (Write on the board:)

> 1. cop   4. card
> 2. cat   5. come
> 3. cot

- All these words begin with the sound **k** spelled with the letter **C**. Look at the words, and we'll spell them together.

b. Word 1 is **cop**. Spell **cop**. Get ready. (Signal.) *C-O-P.*

c. Word 2 is **cat**. Spell **cat**. Get ready. (Signal.) *C-A-T.*

d. (Repeat step c for **cot, card, come.**)

e. When I call on you, see if you can spell the word without looking.

f. (Call on a student.) Spell **cop.** *C-O-P.*

g. (Call on another student.) Spell **cat.** *C-A-T.*

h. (Repeat step *g* for **cot, card, come.**) ✔

EXERCISE 2
SAY THE SOUNDS

a. Listen: **club.** Say it. (Signal.) *Club.*

• Say the sounds in **club.** Get ready. (Tap for each sound.) *k. . . lll. . . uuu. . . b.*

b. What's the first sound in **club?** (Signal.) *k.*

c. Next sound? (Signal.) *lll.*

d. Next sound? (Signal.) *uuu.*

e. Next sound? (Signal.) *b.* Yes, those are the sounds in **club.**

f. (Repeat steps *a–e* for **cold, cloth, cost, spill.**)

g. (Call on individual students to say the sounds in **club, cold, cloth, cost, spill.**)

EXERCISE 3
SENTENCE WRITING

a. Listen to this sentence: **She read the rest of the book.**

b. Say that sentence. Get ready. (Signal.) *She read the rest of the book.*

c. Write the sentence. ✔

d. I'll spell each word. Check your work. Make an **X** next to any word you got wrong.

e. First word: **She.** S-H-E.

f. Next word: **read.** R-E-A-D.

g. (Repeat step *f* for **the, rest, of, the, book.**)

LESSON 147

EXERCISE 1
PATTERNS

a. You're going to spell words that begin with the sound **k** spelled with the letter **C.**

b. Word 1 is **cap.** Spell **cap.** Get ready. (Signal.) *C-A-P.*

c. Word 2 is **cow.** Spell **cow.** Get ready. (Signal.) *C-O-W.*

d. (Repeat step *c* for **can, cub, call.**)

EXERCISE 2
AFFIXES

a. You're going to write words on lined paper. Number your paper from 1 through 4. ✔

b. Word 1 is **call.** What word? (Signal.) *Call.*

• Write the word **call.** ✔

c. Word 2 is **farm.** What word? (Signal.) *Farm.*

• Write the word **farm.** ✔

d. Word 3 is **rock.** What word? (Signal.) *Rock.*

• Write the word **rock.** ✔

e. Word 4 is **sand.** What word? (Signal.) *Sand.*

• Write the word **sand.** ✔

f. (Write on the board:)

> 1. call + ed =
> 2. farm + ed =
> 3. rock + ed =
> 4. sand + ed =

• Now you're going to add **E-D** to these words.

g. After **call** write a plus sign and **E-D.** ✔ After **E-D** write an equal sign. ✔

h. Write a plus sign, and then **E-D,** and then an equal sign to the rest of the words. ✔

i. You're going to add **E-D** to each word to make new words.

j. Word 1 is **called.** What word? (Signal.) *Called.*

• Write the word **called** after the equal sign. ✔

• (Write to show:)

> 1. call + ed = called

• Here's what you should have: **call** plus **E-D** equals **called.**

k. Word 2 is **farmed.** What word? (Signal.) *Farmed.*

• Write the word **farmed** after the equal sign. ✔

l. Word 3 is **rocked.** What word? (Signal.) *Rocked.*

• Write the word **rocked** after the equal sign. ✔

m. Word 4 is **sanded.** What word? (Signal.) *Sanded.*

• Write the word **sanded** after the equal sign. ✔

n. Check your work. Make an **X** next to any word you got wrong.

o. Word 1. Spell **called.** Get ready. (Tap for each letter.) *C-A-L-L-E-D.*

• (Repeat for **2. farmed, 3. rocked, 4. sanded.**)

EXERCISE 3
PROMPTED REVIEW

a. (Write on the board:)

> 1. save
> 2. stand
> 3. every
> 4. call

b. Word 1 is **save.** Spell **save.** Get ready. (Signal.) *S-A-V-E.*

c. Word 2 is **stand.** Spell **stand.** Get ready. (Signal.) *S-T-A-N-D.*

d. (Repeat step c for **3. every, 4. call.**)

e. (Erase the board.)

• Now spell those words without looking.

f. Word 1 is **save.** Spell **save.** Get ready. (Signal.) *S-A-V-E.*

g. Word 2 is **stand.** Spell **stand.** Get ready. (Signal.) *S-T-A-N-D.*

h. (Repeat step g for **3. every, 4. call.**)

i. (Give individual turns on **1. save, 2. stand, 3. every, 4. call.**)

LESSON 148

EXERCISE 1
PATTERNS

a. You're going to spell words that begin with the sound **k** spelled with the letter **C.**

b. Word 1 is **cold.** Spell **cold.** Get ready. (Signal.) *C-O-L-D.*

c. Word 2 is **club.** Spell **club.** Get ready. (Signal.) *C-L-U-B.*

d. (Repeat step c for **cloth, cost, cut.**)

EXERCISE 2
AFFIXES

a. (Write on the board:)

> 1. sand + ed =
> 2. fish + ed =
> 3. salt + ed =
> 4. back + ed =

b. Copy the board. ✔

c. Add **E-D** to make new words. ✔

d. Check your work. Make an **X** next to any word you got wrong.

e. Word 1. Spell **sanded.** Get ready. (Tap for each letter.) *S-A-N-D-E-D.*

• (Repeat for **2. fished, 3. salted, 4. backed.**)

EXERCISE 3
SPELLING REVIEW

a. Get ready to spell and write some words.

b. Word 1 is **cars.** What word? (Signal.) *Cars.*

• Spell **cars.** Get ready. (Signal.) *C-A-R-S.*

• Write it. ✔

c. Word 2 is **charm.** What word? (Signal.) *Charm.*

• Spell **charm.** Get ready. (Signal.) *C-H-A-R-M.*

• Write it. ✔

d. (Repeat step c for **3. friends, 4. backing.**)

e. I'll spell each word. Put an **X** next to any word you missed and write that word correctly.

• (Spell each word twice. Write the words on the board as you spell them: **1. cars, 2. charm, 3. friends, 4. backing.**)

LESSON 149

EXERCISE 1
SPELLING WORDS

a. (Write on the board:)

1. cloth	4. car
2. other	5. glove
3. singing	

b. Word 1 is **cloth.**
• Spell **cloth.** Get ready. (Signal.) *C-L-O-T-H.*
c. Word 2 is **other.**
• Spell **other.** Get ready. (Signal.) *O-T-H-E-R.*
d. (Repeat step c for **3. singing, 4. car, 5. glove.**)
• (Erase the board.)
e. Spell those words without looking.
f. Word 1 is **cloth.**
• Spell **cloth.** Get ready. (Signal.) *C-L-O-T-H.*
g. Word 2 is **other.** Spell **other.** Get ready. (Signal.) *O-T-H-E-R.*
h. (Repeat step g for **3. singing, 4. car, 5. glove.**)

EXERCISE 2
AFFIXES

a. (Write on the board:)

1. fill + ed =
2. belt + ed =
3. last + ed =
4. lock + ed =

b. Copy the board. ✔

c. Add **E-D** to make new words. ✔
d. Check your work. Make an **X** next to any word you got wrong.
e. Word 1. Spell **filled.** Get ready. (Tap for each letter.) *F-I-L-L-E-D.*
• (Repeat for **2. belted, 3. lasted, 4. locked.**)

EXERCISE 3
SENTENCE WRITING

a. Listen to this sentence: **He read some things.**
b. Say that sentence. Get ready. (Signal.) *He read some things.*
c. Write the sentence. ✔
d. I'll spell each word. Check your work. Make an **X** next to any word you got wrong.
e. First word: **He.** H-E.
f. Next word: **read.** R-E-A-D.
g. (Repeat step *f* for **some, things.**)

LESSON 150

EXERCISE 1
SAY THE SOUNDS

a. Listen: **grave.** Say it. (Signal.) *Grave.*
b. Say the sounds in **grave.** Get ready. (Tap for each sound.) *g . . . rrr . . . āāā . . . vvv.*
c. What is the first sound in **grave?** (Signal.) *g.*
d. Next sound? (Signal.) *rrr.*
e. Next sound? (Signal.) *āāā.*
f. Next sound? (Signal.) *vvv.*
Yes. Those are the sounds in **grave.**
g. (Repeat steps *a–f* for **flat, stand, dust.**)
h. (Call on individual students to say the sounds in: **grave, flat, stand, dust.**)

EXERCISE 2
IDENTIFYING SPELLED WORDS

a. I'll spell some words. See if you can tell which word I spell.
b. Listen to this word: **B-O-O-K.**

- What word? (Signal.) *Book.*
c. Listen: **sand.**
- What word? (Signal.) *Sand.*
d. (Repeat step c for **grin, sun, sharp.**)
e. Your turn to spell those words.
f. **Book.** What word? (Signal.) *Book.*
- Spell **book.** Get ready. (Signal.) *B-O-O-K.*
g. **Sand.** What word? (Signal.) *Sand.*
- Spell **sand.** Get ready. (Signal.) *S-A-N-D.*
h. (Repeat step g for **grin, sun, sharp.**)

EXERCISE 3
SPELLING REVIEW

a. Get ready to spell and write some words.
b. Word 1 is **sanded.** What word? (Signal.) *Sanded.*
- Spell **sanded.** Get ready. (Signal.) *S-A-N-D-E-D.*
- Write it. ✔
c. Word 2 is **glove.** What word? (Signal.) *Glove.*
- Spell **glove.** Get ready. (Signal.) *G-L-O-V-E.*
- Write it. ✔
d. (Repeat step c for **3. cost, 4. telling.**)
e. I'll spell each word. Put an **X** next to any word you missed and write that word correctly.
- (Spell each word twice. Write the words on the board as you spell them.)

LESSON 151

EXERCISE 1
SAY THE SOUNDS

a. Listen: **pups.** Say it. (Signal.) *Pups.*
b. Say the sounds in **pups.** Get ready. (Tap for each sound.) *p . . . uuu . . . p . . . sss.*
c. What is the first sound in **pups?** (Signal.) *p.*
d. Next sound? (Signal.) *uuu.*
e. Next sound? (Signal.) *p.*
f. Next sound? (Signal.) *sss.*
Yes. Those are the sounds in **pups.**

g. (Repeat steps a–f for **still, stand, bands.**)
h. (Call on individual students to say the sounds in **pups, still, stand, bands.**)

EXERCISE 2
SPELLING WORDS

a. (Write on the board:)

    1. fished
    2. ringing
    3. farms
    4. sanding
    5. give

b. Word 1 is **fished.**
- Spell **fished.** Get ready. (Signal.) *F-I-S-H-E-D.*
c. Word 2 is **ringing.**
- Spell **ringing.** Get ready. (Signal.) *R-I-N-G-I-N-G.*
d. (Repeat step c for **3. farms, 4. sanding, 5. give.**)
- (Erase the board.)
e. Spell those words without looking.
f. Word 1 is **fished.**
- Spell **fished.** Get ready. (Signal.) *F-I-S-H-E-D.*
g. Word 2 is **ringing.**
- Spell **ringing.** Get ready. (Signal.) *R-I-N-G-I-N-G.*
h. (Repeat step g for **3. farms, 4. sanding, 5. give.**)

EXERCISE 3
SENTENCE WRITING

a. Listen to this sentence: **What is she to do?**
b. Say that sentence. Get ready. (Signal.) *What is she to do?*
c. Write the sentence. ✔
d. I'll spell each word. Check your work. Make an **X** next to any word you got wrong.
e. First word: **What.** W-H-A-T.
f. Next word: **is.** I-S.
g. (Repeat step f for **she, to, do.**)

LESSON 152

EXERCISE 1
IDENTIFYING SPELLED WORDS

a. I'll spell some words. See if you can tell which word I spell.

b. Listen to this word: **B-U-S.**

• What word? (Signal.) *Bus.*

c. Listen: **H-A-V-E.**

• What word? (Signal.) *Have.*

d. (Repeat step *c* for **farm, book, ball.**)

e. Your turn to spell those words.

f. **Bus.** What word? (Signal.) *Bus.*

• Spell **bus.** Get ready. (Signal.) *B-U-S.*

g. **Have.** What word? (Signal.) *Have.*

• Spell **have.** Get ready. (Signal.) *H-A-V-E.*

h. (Repeat step *g* for **farm, book, ball.**)

EXERCISE 2
SPELLING WORDS

a. (Write on the board:)

> 1. salted
> 2. save
> 3. parting
> 4. singing
> 5. some

b. Word 1 is **salted.**

• Spell **salted.** Get ready. (Signal.) *S-A-L-T-E-D.*

c. Word 2 is **save.**

• Spell **save.** Get ready. (Signal.) *S-A-V-E.*

d. (Repeat step *c* for **3. parting, 4. singing, some.**)

• (Erase the board.)

e. Spell those words without looking.

f. Word 1 is **salted.**

• Spell **salted.** Get ready. (Signal.) *S-A-L-T-E-D.*

g. Word 2 is **save.**

• Spell **save.** Get ready. (Signal.) *S-A-V-E.*

h. (Repeat step *g* for **3. parting, 4. singing, 5. some.**)

EXERCISE 3
SENTENCE WRITING

a. Listen to this sentence: **When are we calling?**

b. Say that sentence. Get ready. (Signal.) *When are we calling?*

c. Write the sentence. ✔

d. I'll spell each word. Check your work. Make an **X** next to any word you got wrong.

e. First word: **When. W-H-E-N.**

f. Next word: **are. A-R-E.**

g. (Repeat step *f* for **we, calling.**)

LESSON 153

EXERCISE 1
WORD COMPLETION

a. (Write on the board:)

> 1. d _ _ s
> 2. ha _ _
> 3. the _ _

b. Copy the board. ✔

c. One or more letters are missing from these words. You're going to write the missing letters.

d. Word 1 is supposed to be **does.** What word? (Signal.) *Does.*

• Fill in the blanks so that the word spells **does.**

e. Word 2 is supposed to be **have.** What word? (Signal.) *Have.*

• Fill in the blanks so that the word spells **have.**

f. (Repeat step *d* for **3. these.**)

g. Get ready to spell the words you just wrote.

h. Look at word 1.

• What word? (Signal.) *Does.*

• Spell **does.** Get ready. (Signal.) *D-O-E-S.*

• Fix it if it's not spelled right.

i. (Repeat step *h* for **2. have, 3. these.**)

EXERCISE 2
SPELLING WORDS

a. (Write on the board:)

> 1. standing
> 2. banded
> 3. calls
> 4. five
> 5. those

b. Word 1 is **standing.**
- Spell **standing.** Get ready. (Signal.) *S-T-A-N-D-I-N-G.*

c. Word 2 is **banded.**
- Spell **banded.** Get ready. (Signal.) *B-A-N-D-E-D.*

d. (Repeat step *c* for **3. calls, 4. five, 5. those.**)
- (Erase the board.)

e. Spell those words without looking.

f. Word 1 is **standing.**
- Spell **standing.** Get ready. (Signal.) *S-T-A-N-D-I-N-G.*

g. Word 2 is **banded.**
- Spell **banded.** Get ready. (Signal.) *B-A-N-D-E-D.*

h. (Repeat step *g* for **3. calls, 4. five, 5. those.**)

EXERCISE 3
SENTENCE WRITING

a. Listen to this sentence: **Where are the dogs?**

b. Say that sentence. Get ready. (Signal.) *Where are the dogs?*

c. Write the sentence. ✔

d. I'll spell each word. Check your work. Make an **X** next to any word you got wrong.

e. First word: **Where.** W-H-E-R-E.

f. Next word: **are.** A-R-E.

g. (Repeat step *f* for **the, dogs.**)

LESSON 154

EXERCISE 1
SAY THE SOUNDS

a. Listen: **grin.** Say it. (Signal.) *Grin.*

b. Say the sounds in **grin.** Get ready. (Tap for each sound.) *g . . . rrr . . . iii . . . nnn.*

c. What's the first sound in **grin?** (Signal.) *g.*

d. Next sound? (Signal.) *rrr.*

e. Next sound? (Signal.) *iii.*

f. Next sound? (Signal.) *nnn.*
Yes, those are the sounds in **grin.**

g. (Repeat steps *a–f* for **duds, suns, club.**)

h. (Call on individual students to say the sounds in **grin, duds, suns, club.**)

EXERCISE 2
SPELLING WORDS

a. (Write on the board:)

> 1. friends
> 2. toys
> 3. does
> 4. many

b. Word 1 is **friends.**
- Spell **friends.** Get ready. (Signal.) *F-R-I-E-N-D-S.*

c. Word 2 is **toys.**
- Spell **toys.** Get ready. (Signal.) *T-O-Y-S.*

d. (Repeat step *c* for **3. does, 4. many.**)
- (Erase the board.)

e. Spell those words without looking.

f. Word 1 is **friends.**
- Spell **friends.** Get ready. (Signal.) *F-R-I-E-N-D-S.*

g. Word 2 is **toys.**
- Spell **toys.** Get ready. (Signal.) *T-O-Y-S.*

h. (Repeat step *g* for **3. does, 4. many.**)

EXERCISE 3
SPELLING REVIEW

a. Get ready to spell and write some words.
b. Word 1 is **wishing.** What word? (Signal.) *Wishing.*
- Spell **wishing.** Get ready. (Signal.) *W-I-S-H-I-N-G.*
- Write it. ✔
c. Word 2 is **some.** What word? (Signal.) *Some.*
- Spell **some.** Get ready. (Signal.) *S-O-M-E.*
- Write it. ✔
d. (Repeat step c for **3. where, 4. give.**)
e. I'll spell each word. Put an **X** next to any word you missed and write that word correctly.
- (Spell each word twice. Write the words on the board as you spell them.)

LESSON 155

EXERCISE 1
IDENTIFYING SPELLED WORDS

a. I'll spell some words. See if you can tell which word I spell.
b. Listen to this word: **S-H-A-R-K.**
- What word? (Signal.) *Shark.*
c. Listen: **S-A-N-D.**
- What word? (Signal.) *Sand.*
d. (Repeat step c for **frog, save.**)
e. Your turn to spell those words.
f. **Shark.** What word? (Signal.) *Shark.*
- Spell **shark.** Get ready. (Signal.) *S-H-A-R-K.*
g. **Sand.** What word? (Signal.) *Sand.*
- Spell **sand.** Get ready. (Signal.) *S-A-N-D.*
h. (Repeat step g for **frog, save.**)

EXERCISE 2
SPELLING WORDS

a. (Write on the board:)

> 1. glove
> 2. picks
> 3. other
> 4. these
> 5. rocking

b. Word 1 is **glove.**
- Spell **glove.** Get ready. (Signal.) *G-L-O-V-E.*
c. Word 2 is **picks.**
- Spell **picks.** Get ready. (Signal.) *P-I-C-K-S.*
d. (Repeat step c for **3. other, 4. these, 5. rocking.**)
- (Erase the board.)
e. Spell those words without looking.
f. Word 1 is **glove.**
- Spell **glove.** Get ready. (Signal.) *G-L-O-V-E.*
g. Word 2 is **picks.**
- Spell **picks.** Get ready. (Signal.) *P-I-C-K-S.*
h. (Repeat step g for **3. other, 4. these, 5. rocking.**)

EXERCISE 3
SPELLING REVIEW

a. Get ready to spell and write some words.
b. Word 1 is **many.** What word? (Signal.) *Many.*
- Spell **many.** Get ready. (Signal.) *M-A-N-Y.*
- Write it. ✔
c. Word 2 is **handed.** What word? (Signal.) *Handed.*
- Spell **handed.** Get ready. (Signal.) *H-A-N-D-E-D.*
- Write it. ✔
d. (Repeat step c for **3. move, 4. does.**)
e. I'll spell each word. Put an **X** next to any word you missed and write that word correctly.
- (Spell each word twice. Write the words on the board as you spell them.)

EXERCISE 1
WORD COMPLETION

a. (Write on the board:)

> 1. _ _ op
> 2. ever _
> 3. f _ _ _

b. Copy the board. ✔

c. One or more letters are missing from these words. You're going to write the missing letters.

d. Word 1 is supposed to be **chop.** What word? (Signal.) *Chop.*

• Fill in the blanks so that the word spells **chop.**

e. Word 2 is supposed to be **every.** What word? (Signal.) *Every.*

• Fill in the blanks so that the word spells **every.**

f. (Repeat step d for **3. fall.**)

g. Get ready to spell the words you just wrote.

h. Look at word 1.

• What word? (Signal.) *Chop.*

• Spell **chop.** Get ready. (Signal.) *C-H-O-P.*

• Fix it if it's not spelled right.

i. (Repeat step h for **2. every, 3. fall.**)

EXERCISE 2
SPELLING WORDS

a. (Write on the board:)

> 1. tall
> 2. where
> 3. shave
> 4. falling
> 5. sanded

b. Word 1 is **tall.**

• Spell **tall.** Get ready. (Signal.) *T-A-L-L.*

c. Word 2 is **where.**

• Spell **where.** Get ready. (Signal.) *W-H-E-R-E.*

d. (Repeat step c for **3. shave, 4. falling, 5. sanded.**)

• (Erase the board.)

e. Spell those words without looking.

f. Word 1 is **tall.**

• Spell **tall.** Get ready. (Signal.) *T-A-L-L.*

g. Word 2 is **where.**

• Spell **where.** Get ready. (Signal.) *W-H-E-R-E.*

h. (Repeat step g for **3. shave, 4. falling, 5. sanded.**)

EXERCISE 3
SPELLING REVIEW

a. Get ready to spell and write some words.

b. Word 1 is **other.** What word? (Signal.) *Other.*

• Spell **other.** Get ready. (Signal.) *O-T-H-E-R.*

• Write it. ✔

c. Word 2 is **friends.** What word? (Signal.) *Friends.*

• Spell **friends.** Get ready. (Signal.) *F-R-I-E-N-D-S.*

• Write it. ✔

d. (Repeat step c for **3. these, 4. wave.**)

e. I'll spell each word. Put an **X** next to any word you missed and write that word correctly.

• (Spell each word twice. Write the words on the board as you spell them.)

EXERCISE 1
SAY THE SOUNDS

a. Listen: **fist.** Say it. (Signal.) *Fist.*

b. Say the sounds in **fist.** Get ready. (Tap for each sound.) *fff . . . iii . . . sss . . . t.*

c. What's the first sound in **fist?** (Signal.) *fff.*

d. Next sound? (Signal.) *iii.*

e. Next sound? (Signal.) *sss.*

f. Next sound? (Signal.) *t.*
   Yes, those are the sounds in **fist.**

g. (Repeat steps *a–f* for **stop, spin, strap.**)

h. (Call on individual students to say the sounds in: **fist, stop, spin, strap.**)

EXERCISE 2
SPELLING WORDS

a. (Write on the board:)

> 1. after
> 2. was
> 3. fishing
> 4. wished
> 5. glove

b. Word 1 is **after.**
 • Spell **after.** Get ready. (Signal.) *A-F-T-E-R.*

c. Word 2 is **was.**
 • Spell **was.** Get ready. (Signal.) *W-A-S.*

d. (Repeat step *c* for **3. fishing, 4. wished, 5. glove.**)
 • (Erase the board.)

e. Spell those words without looking.

f. Word 1 is **after.**
 • Spell **after.** Get ready. (Signal.) *A-F-T-E-R.*

g. Word 2 is **was.**
 • Spell **was.** Get ready. (Signal.) *W-A-S.*

h. (Repeat step *g* for **3. fishing, 4. wished, 5. glove.**)

EXERCISE 3
SENTENCE WRITING

a. Listen to this sentence: **These hens are fat.**

b. Say that sentence. Get ready. (Signal.) *These hens are fat.*

c. Write the sentence. ✔

d. I'll spell each word. Check your work. Make an **X** next to any word you got wrong.

e. First word: **These.** T-H-E-S-E.

f. Next word: **hens.** H-E-N-S.

g. (Repeat step *f* for **are, fat.**)

LESSON 158

EXERCISE 1
IDENTIFYING SPELLED WORDS

a. I'll spell some words. See if you can tell which word I spell.

b. Listen to this word: **C-O-M-E.**
 • What word? (Signal.) *Come.*

c. Listen: **H-A-N-D.**
 • What word? (Signal.) *Hand.*

d. (Repeat step *c* for **when, never.**)

e. Your turn to spell those words.

f. **Come.** What word? (Signal.) *Come.*
 • Spell **come.** Get ready. (Signal.) *C-O-M-E.*

g. **Hand.** What word? (Signal.) *Hand.*
 • Spell **hand.** Get ready. (Signal.) *H-A-N-D.*

h. (Repeat step *g* for **when, never.**)

EXERCISE 2
SPELLING WORDS

a. (Write on the board:)

> 1. farming
> 2. cars
> 3. drove
> 4. salted
> 5. does

b. Word 1 is **farming.**
 • Spell **farming.** Get ready. (Signal.) *F-A-R-M-I-N-G.*

c. Word 2 is **cars.**
 • Spell **cars.** Get ready. (Signal.) *C-A-R-S.*

d. (Repeat step *c* for **3. drove, 4. salted, 5. does.**)
 • (Erase the board.)

e. Spell those words without looking.

f. Word 1 is **farming.**
 • Spell **farming.** Get ready. (Signal.) *F-A-R-M-I-N-G.*

g. Word 2 is **cars.**
 • Spell **cars.** Get ready. (Signal.) *C-A-R-S.*

h. (Repeat step *g* for **3. drove, 4. salted, 5. does.**)

EXERCISE 3
SENTENCE WRITING

a. Listen to this sentence: **The friends read a book.**

b. Say that sentence. Get ready. (Signal.) *The friends read a book.*

c. Write the sentence. ✔

d. I'll spell each word. Check your work. Make an **X** next to any word you got wrong.

e. First word: **The.** T-H-E.

f. Next word: **friends.** F-R-I-E-N-D-S.

g. (Repeat step *f* for **read, a, book.**)

LESSON 159

EXERCISE 1
WORD COMPLETION

a. (Write on the board:)

> 1. a_ _ _
> 2. s_ _d
> 3. t_
> 4. w _ _

b. Copy the board. ✔

c. One or more letters are missing from these words. You're going to write the missing letters.

d. Word 1 is supposed to be **also.**
- What word? (Signal.) *Also.*
- Fill in the blanks so that the word spells **also.**

e. Word 2 is supposed to be **said.**
- What word? (Signal.) *Said.*
- Fill in the blanks so that the word spells **said.**

f. (Repeat step *d* for **3. to, 4. was.**)

g. Get ready to spell the words you just wrote.

h. Look at word 1.
- What word? (Signal.) *Also.*
- Spell **also.** Get ready. (Signal.) *A-L-S-O.*
- Fix it if it's not spelled right.

i. (Repeat step *h* for **2. said, 3. to, 4. was.**)

EXERCISE 2
SPELLING WORDS

a. (Write on the board:)

> 1. rocked
> 2. picking
> 3. love
> 4. walls
> 5. come

b. Word 1 is **rocked.**
- Spell **rocked.** Get ready. (Signal.) *R-O-C-K-E-D.*

c. Word 2 is **picking.**
- Spell **picking.** Get ready. (Signal.) *P-I-C-K-I-N-G.*

d. (Repeat step *c* for **3. love, 4. walls, 5. come.**)
- (Erase the board.)

e. Spell those words without looking.

f. Word 1 is **rocked.**
- Spell **rocked.** Get ready. (Signal.) *R-O-C-K-E-D.*

g. Word 2 is **picking.**
- Spell **picking.** Get ready. (Signal.) *P-I-C-K-I-N-G.*

h. (Repeat step *g* for **3. love, 4. walls, 5. come.**)

EXERCISE 3
SPELLING REVIEW

a. Get ready to spell and write some words.

b. Word 1 is **after.** What word? (Signal.) *After.*
- Spell **after.** Get ready. (Signal.) *A-F-T-E-R.*
- Write it. ✔

c. Word 2 is **where.** What word? (Signal.) *Where.*
- Spell **where.** Get ready. (Signal.) *W-H-E-R-E.*
- Write it. ✔

d. (Repeat step *c* for **3. these, 4. save.**)

e. I'll spell each word. Put an **X** next to any word you missed and write that word correctly.
- (Spell each word twice. Write the words on the board as you spell them.)

110

LESSON 160

EXERCISE 1
SPELLING REVIEW

a. Get ready to spell and write some words.
b. Word 1 is **eve.** What word? (Signal.) *Eve.*
• Spell **eve.** Get ready. (Signal.) *E-V-E.*
• Write it. ✔
c. Word 2 is **cars.** What word? (Signal.) *Cars.*
• Spell **cars.** Get ready. (Signal.) *C-A-R-S.*
• Write it. ✔
d. (Repeat step *c* for **3. said, 4. every, 5. chip, 6. house, 7. never, 8. filling.**)
e. I'll spell each word. Put an **X** next to any word you missed and write that word correctly.
• (Spell each word twice. Write the words on the board as you spell them.)

EXERCISE 2
SENTENCE WRITING

a. Listen to this sentence: **When will she move her book?**
b. Say that sentence. Get ready. (Signal.) *When will she move her book?*
c. Write the sentence. ✔
d. I'll spell each word. Check your work. Make an **X** next to any word you got wrong.
e. First word: **When.** W-H-E-N.
f. Next word: **will.** W-I-L-L.
g. (Repeat step *f* for **she, move, her, book.**)
h. Listen to this sentence: **The fishing was also bad.**
i. Say that sentence. Get ready. (Signal.) *The fishing was also bad.*
j. Write the sentence. ✔
k. I'll spell each word. Check your work. Make an **X** next to any word you got wrong.
l. First word: **The.** T-H-E.
m. Next word: **fishing.** F-I-S-H-I-N-G.
n. (Repeat step *f* for **was, also, bad.**)

PRONUNCIATION GUIDE

Symbol	Pronounced	As in	Voiced or Unvoiced*	Introduced in Lesson
a	aaa	and	v	1, 12
m	mmm	ram	v	4, 11
s	sss	bus	uv	9, 16
ē	ēēē	eat	v	19
r	rrr	bar	v	23
d	d	mad	v	27
f	fff	stuff	uv	31
i	iii	if	v	34
th	ththth	this and bathe (not thing)	v	38
t	t	cat	uv	41
n	nnn	pan	v	44
c	c	tack	uv	48
o	ooo	ox	v	51
ā	āāā	ate	v	58
h	h	hat	uv	61
u	uuu	under	v	64
g	g	tag	v	68
l	lll	pal	v	72
w	www	wow	v	76
sh	shshsh	wish	uv	80

Symbol	Pronounced	As in	Voiced or Unvoiced*	Introduced in Lesson
I	(the word I)		v	88
k	k	tack	uv	92
ō	ōōō	over	v	98
v	vvv	love	v	102
p	p	sap	uv	108
ch	ch	touch	uv	113
e	eee	end	v	118
b	b	grab	v	121
ing	iiing	sing	v	124
ī	īīī	ice	v	127
y	yyy	yard	v	131
er	urrr/errr	brother	v	135
x	ksss	ox	uv	139
oo	oooo	moon (not look)	v	142
J	j	judge	v	145
ȳ	īīī/ȳȳȳ	my	v	149
wh	www or wh	why	v or uv	152
qu	kwww (or koo)	quick	v	154
z	zzz	buzz	v	156
ū	ūūū	use	v	158

*Voiced sounds are sounds you make by vibrating your vocal chords. You do not use your vocal chords for unvoiced sounds—you use air only. To feel the difference between voiced and unvoiced sounds, hold your throat lightly and say the sound *vvv*. You will feel your vocal chords vibrating. Then, without pausing, change the sound to *fff*. The vibrations will stop. The only difference between the sounds is that the *vvv* is voiced and the *fff* is not.